D0302126

Listening to four year olds

How they can help us plan their education and care

Jacqui Cousins

WITHDRAWN

the national
early years
network

LIVERPOOL JMU LIBRARY

3 1111 01002 2158

The National Early Years Network
77 Holloway Road
London N7 8JZ
tel 020 7607 9573

© National Early Years Network 1999

ISBN 1 870985 50 8

Designed by Susan Clarke for Expression, IP23 8HH

No part of this publication may be reproduced,
stored in a retrieval system or transmitted, in
any other form or by any means, electronic,
mechanical, photocopying or otherwise without
the express permission of the publishers.

The publication of this book was supported by
awards from the National Lottery Charities
Board and the Vicky Hurst Trust.

Contents

Acknowledgements

To listen to young children is always a pleasure but I am touched that so many children, their families and other educators took me and my questions seriously and gave me so much time. Thank you all, and especially Sonnyboy, your family and all other Travellers – and to Chris, Sonnyboy's wonderful reception teacher who has become such a loyal friend.

Thank you, Noel, for listening as speech was often painfully transformed to writing, and then for reading every single word. Thank you Rose, my mum, who has more common sense than anyone else I know.

Thank you Wendy Scott, Judith Stone, Charles Desforges, Martin Hughes, Mary John, Geva Blenkin and Gillian Pugh, who also took these children of four very seriously and suggested this book. A book cannot be written without a first-class editor. I have found one in Pat Gordon Smith of the National Early Years Network. Thank you.

I am very grateful to other members of the Early Years Language Project team – Mary Chessum, John Gulliver, Graham Hammond, Lorraine Hubbard and Marilyn Goldsbrough – for their contribution to my thinking on this subject and for allowing me to use their material in the preparation of this book. I must make clear that the views expressed here are entirely my own and do not necessarily reflect those of the project team or the opinions of Ofsted.

About the author

An alternative CV adapted by two of the author's grandsons
Jacqui Cousins is an artist and educator who originally studied painting in London and architectural design in Australia. She was once married to Grandad Tony, an adventurous man who lived very dangerously with her and their three sons in the Bush in Australia. She is now married to a gentle potter and painter, Grandad Noel, and has gained two stepchildren and three more children who adopted her when they lost their own mother. She is thus Grandma or Jacqui-Nan to an extended family of 13 boys and one baby girl, and spends much of her life listening to them. We recently described her as 'UN-CON-VEN-SHUN-AL!'

After becoming a young mum and parent-tutor with School of the Air in Australia, Jacqui became fascinated by the minds of infants and retrained to teach children in their early years. For ten years, she taught children aged between three and seven, and eventually became a senior lecturer in early childhood education at Oxford Brookes University. She gained a PhD for two years' study into young children's talking. A further five years was spent on an analysis of their teachers' professional discussions. Those tape recordings of their theorising about children's oral language at four were gathered when Jacqui facilitated their teachers' action research for a year.

That combined experience has enabled Jacqui to listen to young children, their families and other educators in a variety of informal and formal settings.

Desirable outcomes – early learning goals

At the time of going to press, the QCA had concluded its consultation on the 1999 review of the desirable outcomes and it was made clear that what had been known as the 'desirable outcomes' or 'desirable learning outcomes' were to be called early learning goals. All the research featured in this book was completed at a time when the early years field referred only to 'desirable learning outcomes'. These are constantly referred to, and should be taken to be fundamentally the same as early learning goals. In parts of the general discussion, I do refer to 'early learning goals'.

Introduction

The purpose of this book is to highlight the things that four year olds say, how they say them, why they say them and what can be learned from their words – or their silences. Much of the book describes what I personally heard and observed when listening to 130 children aged four and their teachers. I hope that a lot of those experiences can be adapted to settings across the country, and to their individual children and educators.

I used a conversational approach to listen and talk to the children and their educators. In that way, shared meanings and understandings were checked as the conversation proceeded. As might be imagined, the children needed little encouragement to talk because serious research with them became mutually enjoyable. While there were many thoughtful moments, it was also great fun.

Who took part?

Thirty of the children I listened to were in reception classes. Those children, their families and teachers had been taking part in an oral language project set up by Exeter University and Devon LEA. Their parents agreed to them being tape-recorded while taking part in a variety of activities, both indoors and outside. The remaining 100 children were listened to in 1997 and 1998 in the course of my Ofsted inspections of settings for children aged four, or when I was working with them at family centres, arts workshops or at home. They were not tape-recorded.

All the practitioners took part in informal and (later) in more formal reflective discussions with me. Many of them also wrote to me afterwards and their letters provided greater breadth to many of their immediate comments about children aged four. In many cases, the families added their points of view about their children and their learning.

The ethics of conducting research with young children

Respect has been shown to all the children. They knew when they were being tape-recorded or observed, and also that I was aiming to discover why they enjoyed some activities in their settings more than others. Through their prior play with the tape-recorder and the building of a make-believe recording studio, the 30 children who took part in my early research were able to role-play interviews and to ask each other (and me) many questions. Some of those questions were very deep and particularly revealing of their interpretation of the world and their constant search for meaning. Many of these have been included in this book.

Any child or adult who had reservations or felt shy about being tape-recorded was able to switch the recorder off. One child and one adult did so.

The children, families and practitioners gave their informed consent to the tape-recording or written record of our conversations. They all understood clearly that I intended to use their words in a book that would give a 'child's point of view' of their experiences at four. All names except Sonnyboy's have been changed in this book – at his and his family's request, his nickname is retained.

More detail about ethics and carrying out research with young children can be found in several other books and articles.[1]

Recordings linked to observations

While some children and adults talked very fluently, I made detailed notes of the context and developed a technique for transcribing their tape-recorded talk into written form by ignoring overlaps, repeats, pauses and hesitations. This technique enables a story to flow and reveals the child's main preoccupation and the threads of thinking. They and many of the 100 children that I listened to as part of an inspection of their settings initiated spontaneous conversations about their likes and dislikes. I only made notes of the 100, as I was unwilling to add more stress to the inspection process by tape-recording.

I did not ask any of the children direct questions about the adults, but the children generally offered that information as part of their openness and enthusiasm. I was frequently asked about my job and about what I was writing in my book. In all those cases, I made notes of the conversations. My pocket notebook was an essential tool in this research as, without it, some of the tape recordings would not have made sense.

---

1 See: Alderson, P. (1995) *Listening to children: children, ethics and social research*, Barnardo's; David, T. (1992) '"Do we have to do this?": the Children Act 1989 and obtaining children's views in early childhood settings', *Children and Society*, vol. 6, no. 3, pp. 204–211; Miller, J. (1997) *Never too young: how young children can take responsibility and make decisions*, National Early Years Network.

What the research revealed

Extracts of my discussions with the children are included in the text, in particular when they expose the children's construction of their world and the depth of their thinking. An analysis of all the discussions with children has revealed many of their favourite (and less favourite) activities. Observations of the children while engaged in activities showed how enthusiastic they were about learning with their friends and how curious they were about their world. In some cases, observations enabled the identification of those activities most likely to encourage depth in the children's thinking and those which appeared to switch them off.

Analysis of all the discussions with the children's educators revealed how much they all cared about the children and how concerned they were about their education. They also showed how focused they had become upon their interpretations of the 'desirable learning outcomes' (as the 'early learning goals' were known at the time of the research), and how widely these were being misunderstood. Crucially, that analysis has shown how little some educators said they knew about child development and early learning and how unclear they were about the point of child observation with regard to children's learning and their own practice as educators.

1 What's so special about being four?

Sonnyboy: a strong voice for children aged four

On the cover of this book are the words 'time's as long as it takes'. They are taken from a tape-recorded discussion between a reception teacher and one of her youngest pupils, an Irish Traveller child known as Sonnyboy.

At the time of the tape-recording, Sonnyboy was a four year old who could not be ignored. He made everyone think because his words had such a 'ring of truth', with which educators and children alike could identify. Children such as Sonnyboy have the capacity to jolt adults into thinking. That is why, for me, he became a voice for children aged four when they first started school.

As a practitioner–researcher I spent a term in Sonnyboy's reception class studying why some children of four did not appear to talk or use oral language as well at school as they did at home. In the course of that study, Sonnyboy's fluent language and his frequent pearls of wisdom were captured by the radio microphone. Some of the things he said provided me with the clearest insight into the way young children talk to make sense of their world. Listening to Sonnyboy and studying what he said (and how he said it) resulted in the most desirable outcomes: it showed clearly the effect of family and cultural background upon young children's talking, and revealed some of the difficulties some young children experience when they first move away from their family into another social setting. That is particularly relevant now that the age of four appears to be the unofficially acknowledged and accepted age at which our children now start formal schooling in England and Wales.[2]

My observations of Sonnyboy, coupled with discussion with his family and teacher, prompted me to listen even more closely to children aged four and led to this in-depth study of them as young talkers and thinkers. Whether at home or in other settings, Sonnyboy seemed able to speak for many of his peers. He persistently reminded his teacher that the children in her care were 'only four, Miss ... only four!' The shocked tone of Sonnyboy's voice implied they were very young and that was why they were finding school difficult to adjust to.

As his teacher said, 'That really made me think.'

2 Joseph, J. (1993) 'Four year olds in school: cause for concern'. In P. Gammage & J. Meigham, *Early childhood education: taking stock*, Education Now Cooperative.

Through sonic scanning and some exceptional photography and research we now know how the unborn respond to voices and sensory stimulation, such as touch and music.[3] We also know that much of our children's early learning is achieved from birth through sensory exploration and discovery.[4] Nurtured babies are lively and show us how much they need to suck, listen, smell, feel, hear and gain a sense of balance as they begin to move. Their physical responses are observable and the emotional impact can also be assumed by their laughter or tears and other subtleties of their facial expressions and movements.[5] Watching babies at work with treasure baskets shows how capable they are of making early choices and how long they concentrate when they do.

In contrast, extreme conditions in Eastern Europe have shown how abandoned young infants are damaged by being deprived of love and early stimulation. Every possible part of these children's development had been delayed, some of it irreparably so. Poverty and malnutrition have the same effect, as do exposure to excessive stress and anxiety and any form of abuse.

Current work with mobile young infants also shows how much they need to take risks in their pursuit of new knowledge. Videos show how adventurous they are when they feel reassured that it is alright to experiment, create their own problems and solve them, persevere and get things wrong.[6] Much of that early learning is now known to take place in social contexts.[7] Babies may be content to play alongside their friends but they are frequently very interested in each other and communicate from babyhood; in other words, they are born as people – social beings.[8]

Families are the prime educators

The crucial importance of the development of positive self-esteem and self-confidence within the family for successful early learning has been emphasised by the work of Rosemary Roberts.[9] (And in this context, 'the family' includes all variations on the theme of prime carers.)

3 Kitzinger, S. with photographer Nilsson, L. (1986) *Being born*, Dorling Kindersley.
4 Goldschmeid, E. (1987) *Infants at work*, training video, National Children's Bureau.
5 Bower, T. G. R. (1989) *The rational infant*, Freeman.
6 Goldschmeid, E. & Hughes, A., *Heuristic play with objects*, video resource from the National Children's Bureau.
7 Dunn, J. (1988) *The beginnings of social understanding*, Blackwell.
8 Goldschmeid, E. & Jackson, S. (1994) *People under three*, Routledge.
9 Roberts, R. (1995) *Self-esteem and successful early learning*, Hodder & Stoughton.

LIVERPOOL JOHN MOORES UNIVERSITY
LEARNING SERVICES

Sonnyboy and his family

At home in his trailer, Sonnyboy and all his family talked very fluently and confidently. They had been born into an oral culture and nobody in the family could read or write. They had never been to school and their family history and traditional tales were passed down to the young through the skill of their grandparents' and parents' storytelling. It was explained by Sonnyboy's father that, until recently, they had had little need in their lives for reading and writing. He acknowledged that those who had access to the written word in society held the power and control, but he believed they had lost much in becoming too dependent on books rather than on listening to the words of wisdom of older, more experienced people. However, he explained that he now needed to become part of that literate culture because he could not manage to fill in any official forms.

Sonnyboy's two grandfathers are well-remembered for their battles of wit against authority and their far-fetched excuses for staying put on a site. Embellishment of their stories mark them out even today among their own community. Sonnyboy seemed to inherit their talent. He spent a lot of time in his trailer telling stories and entertaining his sister and other younger children. Not all those traditional stories were solely for entertainment. A common way of controlling the younger children (and keeping them safely in their trailers at night) was for the men or the older children to recount stories of fearful dogs, dragons and devils who lived at night in the trees around them.

Sonnyboy invariably brought horses as well as those dogs, devils and dragons into his own stories. He also recounted other stories of ghosts and spirits, which seemed to be derived from a mixture of superstition and the religious faith of his family. These stories frightened some of the other young children at school who cried to the teacher or went home to 'tell my mum about you, Sonnyboy'. That reaction puzzled and upset Sonnyboy because he had only intended to entertain them. His teacher recounted that he became very distressed and sobbed to her that he was 'very, very sorry'. Together they reassured the children. Sonnyboy judged his audience better in the future and even managed to modify some of his stories to provide happy endings.

It was certainly a new experience for Sonnyboy to be in trouble for making other children cry. It went totally against his nature and he had already shown a mature concern for younger and more vulnerable children. It was also part of his family tradition that older siblings were the 'minders' of the young. That spilled over into school and Sonnyboy was frequently heard in the playground trying to stop any taunting or bullying behaviour and inadvertent roughness with 'watch out for the little ones'. Few things made Sonnyboy more angry than bullying; except, perhaps, being interrupted or having to hurry.

In his early days at school, I observed that there were differences in the way Sonnyboy used language compared with other children. For example, he had a very direct way of expressing a point of view. Normally his voice had a very soft and lilting musical timbre. To gain entry to the group discussion his voice changed. He was capable of raising it by an octave and increasing its volume above the teacher and all the children. He was determined to be heard. It was as if his life depended upon it. Perhaps in the distant past it had. In common with many threatened people, the development and use of talk by gypsies over centuries has been concerned with their very survival. Frequently, their voices have been raised but there has been nobody to listen, hear or understand. In spite of an increasing worldwide concern for 'human rights', a majority of nomadic gypsies across Europe live in poverty on the edge of society. They still have to argue their case with officials in order not to be moved on with their trailers before being able or ready to do so.

Sonnyboy had listened from birth to his father arguing about their rights to remain on their particular site, even though that was on the edge of a rubbish dump where no one else wished to be. The officials in that particular city seemed determined to move them on and the youngest boys sometimes became actively involved in those discussions. They even took part with their fathers in some of the financial negotiations associated with the buying and selling of scrap metal found at the dump.

However, in Traveller families there are clear rules for communication with the adults. The young are expected to listen to their elders and not to interrupt or be 'too brazen or bold'. They learn to wait their turn within the family and then to challenge and ask their questions. That is frequently a very direct, physical and noisy procedure. Sonnyboy's father, in particular, expected him (by the age of five) to have a point of view and to argue his case long and hard with the older boys.

Not surprisingly, with that kind of background, Sonnyboy found it difficult at four to adjust to a different way of communicating in his nursery group. He seemed uncertain whether he should treat people at school as family or as officials. When he first started school, he hardly talked to anyone. His teacher described how he had a permanently perplexed expression as he sat silently watching the other children, trying to make sense of what was happening. Despite his exceptional use of language at home, it took Sonnyboy over a month to begin to talk as fluently in class. He had to learn quickly to adapt his normally strong and direct style of communication to a form more socially acceptable to school.

Unlike many other children I listened

to in the course of my research, Sonnyboy was obviously unrushed at home. His family was not ruled by the clock and there was a different rhythm to their lives. Most significantly, I found that any attempt to hurry Sonnyboy or to impose school routines which did not allow him to go into depth with what he was doing or to complete activities to his satisfaction was met with frustration and irritation. This was most notable when 'bells and breaks' interrupted his enjoyment of those activities which required prolonged exploration or needed sustained concentration and perseverance on his part. Examples taken from my observation notebook of Sonnyboy showed how agitated he became when he was stopped in the full flow of telling a story or while absorbed in the exploration of worms or insects in the wild and weedy garden, or while making large constructions with friends in the classroom.

The seemingly carefree 'laid back' attitude – 'time's as long as it takes' – comes straight from the traditional Irish Traveller culture. As Sonnyboy's mother recalled, his grandmother and grandfather had been born in the late 1940s 'in the back of a horse-drawn wagon'. Her whole family had been able to live a leisurely and nomadic life ruled more by the pace of the horses than the fast trucks they drive today. In her opinion, the move away from a nomadic life governed by the slow pace of horses has been responsible for many changes in their culture.

In the past, much of her time had been spent listening to the youngest children in the family and in encouraging them to talk by talking with them. She told me that, in recent years, there had been many changes which had had an effect upon their language. For example, television had made an impact and some traditional families like her own were strict in rationing it for the younger children. She was afraid of its 'corrupting influence' upon their behaviour.

The importance of family culture in social and cognitive development has been stressed by psychologists, including Barbara Tizard and Martin Hughes,[10] Margaret Donaldson[11] and Jerome Bruner,[12] all of whom have examined the development of young children's oral language and thought.

Sonnyboy gave me powerful real evidence of the influence of family and cultural background upon the development of oral language and the process of early learning (see 'Sonnyboy and his family', above).

10 Tizard, B. & Hughes, M. (1984) *Young children learning*, Fontana.
11 Donaldson, M. (1978) *Children's minds*, Fontana.
12 Bruner, J. (1990) *Acts of meaning*, Harvard University Press.

Sharing a common language was seen as more than a simple sharing of words; it was a sharing of culture and a sharing of meaning. Sonnyboy's early learning was embedded in contexts which had meaning for him. He had gained confidence in what he had already come to know and, because he was so strongly supported in secure relationships, he was unafraid of failure.

Children of four certainly appear to benefit from close relationships with those who either share their culture or have a deep knowledge of it. In that way, their learning is embedded in activities, contexts or situations that have meaning for them. Their language develops through everyday spontaneous conversations. As an integral part of those verbal interactions, shared meanings are negotiated and misunderstandings are resolved. With his maturity as a talker, Sonnyboy had become very aware of some of his own misunderstandings and those of other children – and his ability to understand another child's point of view fits current thinking in cognitive and developmental psychology.

Starting school

The age of four is frequently the time when children have to make many social adaptations in order to cope with change. Starting school or going regularly to other settings outside the family is a major upheaval for many. Many children find this an exciting prospect but some find the experience confusing and very tiring. For many who have to contend with too much formality and a developmentally inappropriate curriculum, it is often a stressful time.

Sonnyboy's transitional difficulties in transferring his competence as a communicator to school centred upon the different way talk was used in his family. Some of the difficulties he experienced came about when he misjudged either the audience for his stories (such as the timidity of the younger children) or the new social expectations of the adults (such as waiting his turn and not shouting people down). His early silence at school made his teacher aware of the profound emotional effect such a transition can have upon a sensitive young child's performance as a talker. That loss of self-confidence when he started school at four was dramatic; his teacher knew him to be a good communicator at home because she had visited Sonnyboy's family prior to his starting school. If Sonnyboy struggled in that way, how many other children must there be who suffer in silence? Do people assume that they have little ability to talk?

There is now a large academic literature on children's differing uses of talk and how it might be supported and extended in a variety of settings, including at home. There is an extensive literature on young children's 'transitional' difficulties and about the possible effect of change on their language, emotional development and early learning, particularly when the adults' values, attitudes and norms differ from their own.

Questions, questions

Sonnyboy asked innumerable questions of his very patient teacher and had very strong beliefs about the nature of classroom questions. He lost his sunny smile when she asked questions which, to him, were not real questions which everyone had to puzzle over, but were questions to which the teacher and most of her pupils already knew the answer. In his words to his teacher: 'Why do you keep asking us questions when you know all the answers? Like "What colour is it, then?" You can see for yourself it's red, so why do you keep asking?'

There is no simple answer to Sonnyboy's question. It has been well-researched by Mary Willes that many questions asked of young pupils at school are to test whether the children are listening, paying attention or can provide the teacher with a 'right answer'.[13] They are not intended to help the children in the construction of their own knowledge and are commonly known as 'test' questions.

In my research, the children I listened to were in a variety of settings, so it was possible to ascertain whether that form of 'test' questioning was peculiar to schools and teachers. It was not. Whatever the setting, a majority of adults questioned the children of four in that same 'testing' way. Similarly, during storytimes, many also checked the listening and understanding of their children aged three and, when children's families were consciously taking on the role of educators at home, such as in sharing a book from school, they did the same. Yet when they were being natural with their children, those same parents encouraged the children's own questions and took time to answer them. There is much in Sonnyboy's questioning of the nature of questions for educators to think about and to act upon – perhaps most significantly that he felt emotionally secure enough to challenge his teacher about them.

13 Willes, M. (1988) *Children into pupils: a study of language in early schooling*, Routledge Kegan Paul.

Being emotional and expressing feelings

At one time, it was believed that being able to express feelings is an inevitable part of being a young child. That is no longer seen to be the case. There is concern that, with the demise of extended families, talking about their feelings is no longer part of some young children's everyday lives. At four, some of them may *feel* very emotional but not yet have a language with which to *express* how they feel. They need opportunities to gain that capability because, otherwise, they can become very frustrated and inhibited.

It is now maintained that 'early emotional literacy and emotional intelligence' plays a much larger part in cognition than was originally thought. In particular, the ability to talk through situations and to develop a language for the emotions influences decision-making, risk-taking, the avoidance of being a victim and gaining a sense of success – for life.[14] It is the emotional lessons gained as a young child that can shape the actual circuitry of the brain.

Unlike Sonnyboy, who saw no harm in challenging an adult or in trying new experiences, children who are afraid to take risks as learners because of their anticipation of failure may never achieve their potential as thinkers. Even later into their adulthood, they are likely to remain inhibited about taking any chances or being adventurous. The origins of their sense of failure may well have been long forgotten but the need to run away or escape from challenging situations will still be there in the subconscious. That is the last thing anybody would wish in the shaping of our young people still 'only four!'

Playing with words

At around four, children's talking and understanding of language becomes more sophisticated. They may enjoy playing even more with sounds and making up their own rhyming words. They also begin to realise that there are other meanings for words they know. They discover new explanations for many things through their senses or by asking their family to explain.

By four, Sonnyboy had already begun to connect that different meanings could be ascribed to familiar words. Because he was a very confident and articulate child, this did not worry him and he did not regard not knowing as a sign of failure or weakness. Instead, he saw that

---

14 Goleman, D. (1996) *Emotional intelligence*, Bloomsbury.

Sonnyboy was able to explain some of the different meanings placed on words. For example, when his teacher asked the children for their 'letters', his friend David stood and looked blankly at her and offered the 'name card' he had been given to help him learn his alphabet, or 'letters'. Sonnyboy put an arm round him and whispered, 'Not that sort of letter, David, one on paper what your mum wrote'.

He used anecdotes, stories and 'real' experiences to help David and other children to make sense of what was needed, especially for problem-solving in mathematics. His speed in making mathematical calculations was equally exceptional. He was able to calculate 'in my head' and give change while serving and pouring orange juice into beakers. It was also common to see him helping his friends understand addition and subtraction by counting on his fingers (and theirs) or finding them small toys to count with and checking their understanding with comments like, 'D'you see? D'you see? No, not like that [using blocks]. Get it now? Use them ...three ... one more ... four ... yeah! 1, 2, 3, 4, see? 1, 2, 3, 4 ... right!'

On many occasions I watched as Sonnyboy played with David in setting up the model farm. He used the small animals in separate fields to add, subtract, share hay bales and to calculate how many more bales were needed to feed all the animals. He took his time and told a story about the farm as he solved those problems. Sonnyboy frequently put his arm round David and whispered, 'When you're big you'll understand. Don't you go worrying your head, Dave. You're only four!'

Unlike David, Sonnyboy was unafraid to risk being wrong or not knowing the answers himself. On many occasions he stated to David and to other children that it was 'alright not to know, 'cos you go to school to learn!'

any problems rested firmly with the adult, who would be able to explain.

Closely linked to that expectation was the children's awareness and trust that their 'keyworker' would 'help us to sort things out', which effectively continued the process of negotiating shared meanings and a shared understanding. That process was achieved mainly through talk although, as many of the educators I spoke to said, there is generally too little time for that. For others, supporting the children's reflective discussion is a priority because they find it an effective way to evaluate the children's learning and to discover their individual interests and social capabilities.

Feeling confused

Young children at four (and earlier) can be very confused by moving from setting to setting. This is most noticeable where young children encounter inconsistencies, so that what is acceptable in one setting is not acceptable or is positively discouraged in another. Perhaps what has made so much sense at home no longer seems to make sense in another social situation.

At four or thereabouts, children become aware of some of their own confusion. They begin to realise that something that they previously thought they had known and understood does not make sense any more. Their initial response is through emotions. Depending on the child, they may feel insecure and lose confidence or become anxious, quiet or thoughtful. Some children may feel quite the opposite and be excited and stimulated by the unknown and the new learning adventures ahead of them. Simultaneously, something known as 'cognitive confusion' is provoked by having to face the unknown.

Their 'not knowing' has a strong emotional impact as they begin to feel something is wrong or when they become uncomfortably aware that they have misunderstood something. It throws them temporarily off-balance intellectually and they immediately ask questions to try and confirm what they thought they knew. That subconscious process goes on throughout our lives. Asking questions and receiving satisfactory answers is one of the main mechanisms for human beings to regain 'cognitive equilibrium', or a sense of inner balance or harmony. Whatever their emotional response to the unknown, children of about four become conscious of some of their own misunderstandings and misinterpretations. With that consciousness comes the need to talk. Questions just tumble out. What this research has shown me is how intense that questioning to negotiate a shared meaning becomes at four. Not all young children have the language abilities to express their understandings or to check our meanings with their own. It is part of a maturing process. When facilitating adults listen to them they gain confidence in themselves as communicators in a variety of situations or contexts.

Gentle correction

Sonnyboy had to learn that at school he needed to voice his opinions and ask his questions without being too abrupt, but at home he had to maintain his directness with the other boys in order to hold his own. Like many children of four he lived in many different worlds and had to learn to switch his communication as he moved from one to the other.

Sonnyboy's teacher was one of the most skilled and sensitive people in the art of correcting children while enabling them to remain comfortable and secure. One way she achieved that was by standing absolutely quiet and still to gain attention and then raising her eyebrows in an expression of 'surprise'. That was followed by a clear explanation of the problem to the child or group involved. One of her children described her as having 'a softy voice'. She managed Sonnyboy's transitional difficulties (and all the other children's) without any unnecessary tension or shouting, often simply with a hug and gentle humour. I found it moving to hear Sonnyboy checking at his early stage of settling at school, 'That wasn't rude was it? I wasn't being a bit brazen and bold was I, Miss? If I was, I'd say sorry.' He adapted his language very quickly and was never rude or lacking in respect.

Why, why, why?
Scaring people by asking 'why'?

Sonnyboy often questioned his teacher and asked her 'why', as in the example above where he asked her 'Why do you keep asking us questions when you know all the answers?' He did not mean to be 'brazen or bold' when asking these questions, but they sounded very different from other times when, like many other children he would 'wonder why' something was as it was. The former often sounded confrontational and challenging while the latter was much gentler in tone. As counsellors, child therapists or humanistic psychologists such as Denis Lawrence have written,[15] being faced with a small child (or anybody else) who asks 'why?' can feel very threatening. To the insecure, the question 'why?' constitutes a challenge to adult authority and, for an educator, to the control of the group. The power at that moment shifts to the child, and many teachers lack the confidence to let go and allow an open discussion of controversial or puzzling issues. Fear of losing control is a very human response.

In addition, it can be very exhausting to continually rephrase the answers to a child's 'why?' in such a way that the child will understand and the other children will remain attentive. Remaining attentive and listening to the adult is a large part of many children's day in whichever setting they happen to be. Other children might lose the thread of the task in hand and distract the group which, in turn, becomes restless. Many children told me that they did not like 'being all squashed together on the carpet ... in the book corner ... but we've got to learn to listen'. One educator was very concerned about a boy of

---

15 Lawrence, D. (1987) *Enhancing self-esteem in the classroom*, Paul Chapman Publishers.

almost five. He kept interrupting her and asking 'why?' She explained:

I can't spend all day listening to him ... he interrupts the flow. It takes a long time to explain everything to the group ... I want them to get on with their work otherwise they'll never reach all their desirable outcomes by five. He has to wait his turn to ask.

Some children are able to wait their turn to ask their questions, but some simply cannot do so at four or even much later. Their questions often come spontaneously from their own action or that around them and, without any hesitation, spring straight from the subconscious to their voice. The child referred to in that example was one of the most original and creative thinkers in that setting, but I suspect that receiving this constant rebuttal from his teacher was having a very detrimental affect on his social behaviour. Rather than learn to control himself, I watched him 'lash out at the world' in sheer frustration. To date, there is too little support given to young children who are this intelligent. That child needed his own keyworker or an adult who could listen to him directly for at least part of his time in the setting. Academically, he was way past all his early learning goals, but socially he still needed considerable support. His case was not unique.

Wondering 'why'?

Like most young children, when he first started school Sonnyboy was more used to 'proper questions ... you know, about life and that'. Researchers into cognition all identify the age of four as significant for children's most persistent intellectual curiosity. Depending upon their all-round maturity, some children as young as three ask many questions. It is a process which should continue for life – but intellectual curiosity is individual and seems to depend on many other factors, such as how children's early questions were responded to. Researchers have all noted how constantly children of four wonder 'why' in their conversations, as a natural part of human sense-making.

In my research, the children asked some of their deepest questions about ordinary everyday things rather than about set tasks, games or activities. Often they are very funny, sometimes profound and very sad. Some questions asked by children are deeply intellectual despite being (in the main) about everyday things. It is always interesting to listen to them and to have a pocket book in which to jot them down. Here are a few questions I heard:

- How does that (soap dispenser in the playgroup) work?
- Where does water go when it goes down the drain?
- What does that label (on a jacket) say? Why does it keep me warm?

- Do underwater people in special masks paint the sea its different colours?
- Do butterflies use their wings like umbrellas to keep themselves dry in the rain?
- Where do worms go when the snow is on the ground? Can they breathe?
- How does a maypole work? Is that thing at the top called a rat-shit? Why?
- Why do people call them things water melons 'stead of juicy melons?
- Do daddies ever come back when you never, never knowed them ever?

Thirty years ago, the late Connie Rosen supported my earliest formal study into the oral language of reception children in Haringey, London.[16] She encouraged all her students to provide plenty of opportunities for the children's spontaneous enquiry and to add tape-recording to our child observations. She gave us very sound advice: 'Try to evoke a sense of wonder in your classes, then your young children will be encouraged to ask questions and thus develop their minds.'

In 1999, Connie's advice has even greater relevance. To wonder 'why' is a natural phenomenon of childhood, particularly around the age of four. In my current research even those practitioners who had taken such trouble to set up excellent 'interest or discovery' areas did not recognise their true value in terms of encouraging children's thought. Our pioneers in early education certainly understood the significance of young children's questioning. Those of us who share their beliefs and their vision for young children have had the benefit of a more sophisticated technology to prove them right. Tape-recording can often be very revealing of how many questions we ask. One child in my research listened to himself on the tape recorder and said to me: 'I never knew I asked so many questions. Do they stretch my thinking brain?' Young children have their own way of expressing such profound thoughts. No doubt neurologists would be able to answer that child's question. He certainly did ask a lot and so did the adults in his setting. When they listened to their tapes they were very surprised by their frequency.

The underlying reasons for questioning to be so intense at four are very complex. Personality and the essence or spirit of the child certainly cannot be ignored in that process; neither can the children's physical development. With increasing mobility and a strong sense of

---

16 Rosen, C. & Rosen, H. (1973) *The language of primary school children*, Penguin.

adventure their horizons are expanded and they face many new and puzzling things to ask questions about. As their talking becomes more sophisticated they need to check out their own constructions and interpretations of their world. Still more questions are associated with the development of their emotions and the impact made upon them in their extending relationships with their peers, friends and others inside and outside the family.

Imitating others

As well as copying our own and each other's behaviour, children frequently look around to see how their friends are responding to different people and to the various learning situations.

Watching children at role play in the home area was particularly enlightening for me; the unequal division of labour was evident, with girls still slaving over cooking stoves while the boys lounged around waiting to be waited on. Sometimes they gave the pram a token rock with a lazy toe. Some staff tried to address those gender issues but, on the whole, those patterns went unnoticed.

In one setting some of the children had become so interested in their keyworker's observations and in 'the Ofsted lady's' notebook that they had made small books of their own. Some sat nearby and observed me. I was able to give them all their desirable outcome ticks in all the areas but especially for social development. I was very interested in their comments and their intelligent questions about my job. Emma was particularly curious and her own notebook was full of her own emergent writing. She pointed to her writing as she read out her comments word by word. Then she spotted an E in among my writing and asked:

[Looking over my shoulder] *Why do Ofsted ladies always have to write a lot? What does that say? I think it says E ... Emma-is-a-lovely-little-girl ... she-is-very-clever! Right? I know really it doesn't say Emma 'cos I can write my name ...I'll show you ...* [sounding out the word] *big E-m- and another m and a for apple ... see?*

Another child in my earlier research had strong views about not wishing to be tape-recorded. He felt it would be intrusive because it was 'all my private stuff'. I agreed not to do so and he went off happily to the home area. He then proceeded to have an argument with 'the wife' but called to me: 'I'm only pretending.' He did not mind my other observations but asked what I would do with them: 'Will you write all those words in your book or will you cut them into bits and give them to our mums and dads ... like an MOT? ... We just got one a them.'

What an imaginative idea to give all the children MOT certificates and to cut all my notebooks up and distribute the bits to the most relevant people, the 'mums and dads'! In my own observations I included those natural and spontaneous questions because they give such insight into the children's puzzling minds.

Builders of knowledge and experience

That young child was verbalising as he matched his old knowledge to something which puzzled him, and thus he constructed his new knowledge. Young children's constructions of the world are frequently very different from those of adults. That is why we can confuse them so much when we impose our adult ideas upon them. It is often quite difficult to follow the children's line of thought because, as adults, we have passed that stage of thinking.[17] It takes imagination to visualise the world from their point of view.

I noticed that it was those educators who were able to empathise with their children and were skilled in listening who encouraged reflective discussion and the deepest questions. By four, children are able to build upon their extending experiences and, with our help, are able to articulate their own profound theories about all manner of things.

Developing as logical and imaginative thinkers

I found questions like, 'What made you say that?', 'Why do you think that?', 'Do you mean...?' and 'I wonder what you were thinking then' often provoked some of the children's most thoughtful comments and helped them to reveal the way they saw the world. It takes time, but reflective dialogue with supportive adults is essential if our young children are to extend their capacity to use their language creatively and to reason. A key factor is to link closely with what they say.

I will include only one example from my research, which I wrote initially as a story before reorganising it for academic purposes into case study form. In the course of my research I was able to collect dozens more such stories of life as it is lived with young children.

---

17 Nutbrown, C. (1994) *Threads of thinking: young children learning and the role of early education*, Paul Chapman; Nutbrown, C. (ed.) (1996) *Respectful educators, capable thinkers*, Paul Chapman.

Dean, aged four: a logical and imaginative thinker

This is a summary of a story about Dean. It includes a section taken from a long spontaneous conversation I had with him.

Dean's teacher had been very concerned about him because he had not talked to anybody in her reception class since he started school two weeks earlier. Like Sonnyboy, he was a child who sat and watched, but unlike Sonnyboy he looked very, very sad. In my visits to the teacher's setting as her support teacher, I had not seen Dean talking or making any contact with other children. Despite close contact with the teacher and very gentle settling in by his mother, he seemed to be fretting and could not be drawn into the group. By chance, I watched him in the playground and saw Dean bend down and peep through the railings to look longingly at his old nursery. The children were just going out for a walk and I could see two big tears rolling silently down his cheeks. Clearly, he was missing his friends very much and when I picked him up he just clung to me and sobbed. Would he like to go back to the nursery for a visit, I asked. His crying stopped when his teacher agreed. The change in Dean when we stepped through the nursery door was instantaneous and I captured it all on my mini tape-recorder.

The children were still out having their walk, so Dean rushed round and round the nursery touching familiar toys and looking in cupboards and on shelves. He talked non-stop and when he spotted the indoor pond full of fish and tadpoles he remembered all the details of going to collect them and building the pond with his nursery nurse. At one point his face moved close to the water and he peered through a magnifying glass:

D: What that thing? That a fish?

JC: Mmm … Think so … Can't really see it for all the weeds.

D: Fish got eye flaps?

JC: Got what, Dean?

D: Eye flaps, like my…? *[points to his own eyelids; I laugh with Dean].*

JC: Eyelids – I like your name 'eye flaps'… I don't really know. What made you ask that question, Dean?'

D: That fish sleep. Look … look, him fast asleep but he never shut him eyes.

JC: Why do you think he's asleep? He might just be watching. His eyes are open.

D: No, no, him sleep 'cos …'cos … fishy not move him tail … he stop still in the weeds, in the weeds.

Despite Dean's earlier reticence and some immaturity in his speech, that short episode reveals something of his capacity as a logical and imaginative thinker. He closely observed a fish and asked his question about 'eye flaps', and the ensuing discussion revealed the thinking behind that question. He had noticed that the fish was not moving ('fishy not move him tail') so he guessed that it might be asleep.

However, he had noticed that the fish's eyes were wide open, and this went against Dean's existing knowledge that eyes close when we sleep. Some confusion occurred and he looked puzzled. Dean's next comment shows that his uncertainty could be resolved if, in fact, fish do not have eyelids; hence his very intelligent question. His invention 'eye flaps' is imaginative, and the language which Dean used in that brief moment made the highest possible demands on his thinking. He spoke with no hesitation.

When she listened to the tape later, Dean's teacher was delighted to have found the cause of his distress and to discover how well he talked. I suspected that some of the dramatic change in Dean's language flow could also be attributed to a sudden release from emotional tension. The depth of his distress and the emotional impact on him of leaving his nursery too soon had had a profound effect. When his teacher observed other children in her youngest group she thought that they too would benefit from more time in the nursery. The staff rearranged their weekly programmes so that they too could enjoy a more appropriate environment. She found their enjoyment of school and their questions increased.

Becoming even more 'brainy'

More is now being discovered about the brain and the deep interconnection between its development and the development of emotions or feelings. It is now known that damage or delay to one can profoundly affect the other and this in turn can have an effect on the whole development of the person for life. Many educators who I listened to in the course of my research knew that their children's development was still at a very early stage at four and that the 'wiring' of their brain is incomplete.

That incomplete 'wiring' can be compared to an electrician having many loose threads of thin wire that need to be soldered or sealed to complete each circuit. We can imagine the same state inside the brain. Its incomplete and flexible structure has many loose 'wires' or unsealed neurons. Talk and action spark off the sealing of concepts. Unsealed neurons provide an immature mechanism for thinking, or an immature conceptual framework. That word 'immature' is of very great significance because it does not in any way suggest that there is something wrong with those children – their development is perfectly normal. To try and rush them into abstractions before essential parts of their circuitry are complete is likely to confuse and distress them.

Excessive time spent in practising mature skills ironically does not help them to mature. It actually hinders them because their muscles, minds and emotions pull against the process; and we can imagine what happens to the spirit. Once negative emotions take hold, it has been found how many of our youngest children become disaffected too early with the exciting journey of education, a journey that should last a lifetime.[18]

Similar arguments were presented as far back as 1897, and close observation of young children's physical movement was already providing a good clue to the workings of their brain.[19] That early research project with doctors and teachers working together went on until the late 1930s, but was interrupted by World War II.

18 Barrett, G. (ed.) (1989) *Disaffection from school? The early years*, Falmer Press.
19 Dr Warner, Senior Physician at the London Hospital (1897) *The study of children*, Macmillan.

2 What we learn from listening to four year olds

Listening to children and observing them go side by side. They are inseparable because, without observation, much of what children say would not make sense. In carrying out my research, I observed children as an outsider who did not belong to their settings, making my experiences fundamentally different from the ones that most practitioners would have. However, I hope the lessons I learnt about the interests, preferences and concerns of four year olds can provide a secure foundation on which practitioners can build their own understanding of the children in their care – and respond to their true needs. In all settings, everywhere, we can watch, listen and learn from the children.

What an observer hears and sees

In the course of my research, watching the children provided insights into their talk and showed what they were really doing rather than what I thought or imagined they were doing. Those incidental observations were usually spontaneous and provided snapshots of moments in the children's lives. While snapshot observations were valuable in giving an impression of what was taking place as the children engaged in different activities, without discussion with people who really knew the children they would only have been superficial.

Part of being an outsider meant that I did not fully understand all the routines and influences upon the children's talk and action. To interpret child observations in greater depth, I needed some insider knowledge which only the children's families and staff could provide. It was particularly enlightening to have many different people in a setting give me their own observations of the same children. Certainly, family contributions and earlier treasured items such as 'baby books' and albums of 'favourite people and favourite things' were invaluable. Many of those included photographs which showed their children's development and included tapes of some of their children's early talking and videos of special events. It was items like that which made me feel that I already knew the children.

I found the children behaved and responded differently with different people in their settings. To give an example, I found a child in my earlier research who said nothing inside his nursery but, when he was tape-recorded in conversation with the caretaker in the garden, he stood next to him and explained some of the most complicated details about the scaffolding he could see around a building: 'That's strong scaffold … thingie … Look, look up. You need a triangle like that *[pointing to a strut]* … one, two, three. Did you know triangles are very, very strong?'

Once his keyworker heard that tape-recording she ceased to worry about his oral language but allowed him more time to play with the construction sets which clearly interested him. Her next observation showed how well he was building a bridge with a group of friends and how much his confidence had grown – he was talking to them non-stop. The boy's mother was not surprised by his knowledge, as she herself was a structural engineer. Later, the teacher used samples of this child's high-quality language and depth of thinking in her own work-based research of the children.

When I listened to the children's educators I found a great deal of anxiety about child observation and the time it took. While most practitioners saw the point in terms of the children's responses to activities, some said they knew too little about early childhood development to be able to relate their observations to the children's learning or to the support they were giving in that process. That has crucial implications for training in the early years and I will return to this subject in Section 3. For now, it is time to listen to the children.

What four year olds like – and dislike

Overwhelmingly, irrespective of the setting, the children's relationships with adults and friends were of fundamental importance to them. I noticed that when the children gave details about events or activities that they had particularly enjoyed, some of them could hardly keep still. Little hands flapped and happiness seemed to burst out of them as they looked at the photographs and remembered shared times with their friends. I found that many children talked more about the people who were involved in those activities than the details of the activities themselves. From what they said, it appeared that their relationships to the adults with them were key to their whole learning experience, colouring their attitudes towards themselves as learners and probably determining what they actually learnt.

Children of four are social beings, so it would be unusual for them to talk about their favourite activities without reference to other children or adults. They also spontaneously included in our discussions about people the things they did not like – and most of those negative views were more their reflections on general situations in their settings rather than remarks about specific people.

The remainder of this section looks at what the children said on the subject of the themes or types of activity that emerged as clear favourites among the four year olds I observed and which they spoke about most frequently. Those nine favourites are:

1 people who love us and teach us lots of things;
2 people who are calm and sort out big bullies;
3 playing with friends and having fun;
4 cooking food and feasting together;
5 finding out about different people;
6 finding out about all sorts of things;
7 beautiful books, stories and learning to read and write;
8 playing at shops, building with bricks and making patterns and shapes; and
9 painting, collage and making lots of models.

The discussion of each area will include children's words and intersperse critical observations. Children were so clear about 'things I don't like people doing' that I have included their main concerns after looking at more positive aspects of educators' relationships with them. All the children's views, experiences and behaviour given here are intended here as signposts to good practice – ways of helping all practitioners interpret the needs of the children in their care and to provide for those needs.

1 | People who love us and teach us lots of things

In all the settings, a majority of the children said with feeling how much they enjoyed being there and followed it immediately with how much they liked their 'teachers'. In the larger settings, the children referred to all the adults as 'teacher' and began many of their discussions with: 'Teacher ... Look! ... Teacher, look at this!' Many children described the work of the adults as 'teaching us lots of things, like reading and all our alphabet'. Some children had underestimated how long it might take to become fluent readers. They expressed disappointment that they had not managed it on their first day but were as confident as the child who said 'teacher helps me with all that stuff'. Helping the children was high on their list of attributes for adults in their settings.

Without any prompting, the children volunteered full descriptions of what they liked most about those adults. Of vital importance seemed to be kindness and being looked after by a smiling and fair person who loved them and helped them if they fell over. They used the word 'love' often and with great feeling. The children needed to feel safe and secure in their relationships with their educators and enjoyed being praised for their efforts.

Patsy embodies the sentiments of many of the children. As she painted a picture of her first 'teacher', she said:

> MY ... TEACHER ... This is my teacher with her happy face and she's very very kind and I like her because she's all green and I like green ... and she's very kind to little children when they talk and talk and take long to ask her things ... and she can say never mind ... ah ... never mind in a softy voice and never, never shout.

Children invariably talked to me with great affection about their own teacher or keyworker, particularly when they explained some of the routines in their setting, such as listening to a story in a small group. One little boy provided many details:

> We all got a keyworker. Kathy, well, she's the boss. She collects all the money on Mondays. But Ann ... I love Ann ... Ann's my special keyworker and we have a little group ... [holding up five fingers and counting] one, two, three, four, five, that how many ... five ... Ann looks after all of us and helps us with our work. Jenny looks after another group ... and Paul ... then Kathy ... Kathy has us all together. We have to tidy up when Kathy says but Ann helps us to put everything away, then we tell her what we just done and what we found out all morning. Then it's story. We go to our own corner ... it's peace and quiet time ... then Ann talks to our mums and then we go home ... or ... I go to ... up Deb's place.

That child was coping well with the various routines and activities. In common with all the children in his group, he had positive attitudes towards learning and about himself as a learner. Like Sonnyboy, when I observed them those children were not afraid to experiment or risk being wrong. They had Sonnyboy's conviction that they go to school to learn and it was alright not to know things, because the teachers were there to teach them. Some of the children I observed struggling with tasks were a long way from that degree of confident faith in the adults. They still needed a great deal of emotional support and time to settle and adapt to the succession of people who came on different days to their settings. For some of them it was all very confusing. Their puzzled frowns showed their perplexity.

As I will explain later, many of the children moved to other settings each afternoon. Had it been possible, it would have been preferable for them to stay in one place and be able to relate to one main person who got to know them and their areas of strength or struggle very well.

LIVERPOOL JOHN MOORES UNIVERSITY
LEARNING SERVICES

Those children who seemed least secure did not have any one adult in either setting such as those described so affectionately earlier by that child as his 'special keyworker'.

It is not only the children who feel insecure who need emotional support as they develop as enthusiastic and confident learners. As the comments of children in the next section reveal, some were very aware of their own need for calm.

2 | People who are calm and sort out big bullies

It was rather surprising to hear so many children of four talk about their enjoyment of people who were calm and gave them plenty of 'peace and quiet'. Ann, mentioned earlier by a boy in her group, was such a person. He may have heard adults using that expression but when listened to it was clear that he and many other children knew exactly what they meant. One mature little boy of four years ten months probably echoed his mother as he told me:

> You simply can't spend all your time rushing around and making a big noise ... Mummy said my batteries would run down. We haven't really got batteries, but Mummy means inside me will get tired ... worn out like her nerves ... they get all worn out when my little brother screams and screams.

Peace, quiet and comforting things

Without exception, children commented upon and responded very positively to any quiet areas in their settings. Clearly these were special and were treated so. In a few settings the imaginative staff had made a point of providing the young children with a softly furnished space in which to be quiet, calm and reflective. An adult spoke to me about a small area in a corner of the room. She described its as 'a soft cave for the children's inner being. I enjoy sitting there for five minutes thought when I have a chance ... I watch the children from there.'

In her 'cave', the pastel colours, natural materials, perfumed flowers and herbs and soft draping of the sheltering screen, mats and cushions helped to create an atmosphere of calm. Boisterous physical play sometimes went on in an adjoining area. This was certainly not the ideal. The children themselves realised that – a group of girls asked whether they could move the noisy bricks further away and then did so with the help of two of the boys who thought it 'a good idea'.

In a similar setting, which also included children aged three, the staff and families had agreed that, irrespective of their various faiths, respect should be shown for the spirituality or inner life of all the children. The children responded clearly to this, showing respect for each other, for the adults around them and for visitors. In other settings, the children (and adults) could find nowhere quiet to be. Some created their own space, as the following observation reveals.

I was in a very stimulating reception class with one teacher, an assistant, a parent helper and 34 children. The room was very small and seemed to be full of furniture, noise and restlessness. The play area outside was used only for organised physical education and for playtimes. I was listening to some of the children aged four when I saw one of them crawl under a table. She held a cushion and dragged a teddy bear and shawl behind her. As I continued to listen to the children, I could see she had made herself and the bear very comfortable and had settled down with her hands over her ears. At playtime she came out and smiled in my direction. I wondered whether she was well and must have looked concerned because she said, 'I'm not ill. Me and my teddy's listening to the peace.'

Having her teddy bear and the soft shawl as comfort objects was very important to her. Security and comfort mattered similarly to many other children of four. In their discussions with me they associated being allowed to keep their talisman of comfort as a sign of the care of 'very kind people' who looked after them. There were often misunderstandings by the children's families about whether or not the children were allowed to take their 'cuddlies' or (as one mother said) 'his precious bit of old rag' to their settings.

Each individual I listened to on that subject revealed misunderstandings or misinterpretations of the settings' rules. In none were four year olds *forbidden* to take them. In most settings, the children were asked not to bring their own toys because they might get lost or spoilt, except on special occasions like birthdays or for a particular project. They were asked to put their comfort objects in a safe place (usually a special box or basket) when they felt ready to part with them. Many children did so but those who could not had no pressure put on them. In the main, the setting staff appeared to have realistic expectations for the emotional maturity of the children. They were more understanding and tolerant of their need for such comfort than some of the families who seemed either embarrassed by the tattiness of the objects or fearful that it was a sign that their child was too insecure or immature. Somehow they associated a child's need for comfort as a sign of their own failure as parents. In many instances they actually told their children that they were not allowed by the teachers to keep them because by four they had got to grow up. Some of the children talked about other children laughing or teasing them because they needed a comforter and families said they wanted to protect their children from feeling distressed.

Responding well to bullies and difficult behaviour

The issue of being laughed at or teased emerged again when the children talked about 'bullies' as people they disliked. In many of the larger urban settings many of them, like this girl, shuddered and said to me: 'I'm frighted of big bullies.'

A majority of the children had never experienced actual bullying, but they had heard about bullies from other people. They seemed afraid of possible bullying by 'bigger kids' but had no fear of it from adults. I will expand on this subject when I discuss the kinds of people the children did not like in their various settings (see pp. 35–40). What they *did* like was the absolute certainty that their 'teachers' (or 'my mum' or 'my dad') would 'soon sort big bullies out'.

The unquestioning confidence that their problems would be sorted out by 'teacher' was equated by the children with specific rules of their setting and being listened to by people who took them seriously. It seemed important to the children to have clear rules as well as reassurance. Many knew exactly who to talk to if they were upset or worried or if one of the younger children got hurt. Most children, with the help of the adults in their settings, were able to talk in their groups about their fears, including those about bullying. Together they established clear boundaries of what was individually tolerable and socially acceptable. Some children showed me charts they had made with the adults and had stuck on their wall. They sometimes called them 'OUR OWN RULES' and they focused on positive aspects of life in their settings which made them happy to be there.

In a majority of settings, the children showed me story books and puppets that, as one child said, 'my kind teacher bringed in specially'. They were used in 'group times' to help the children talk about any frightening or disturbing things. Recently, I have noticed an increasing number of settings that have adopted very positive and systematic approaches to the development of personal self-confidence and the prevention of aggression through learning how to negotiate.

As a specific part of their responsibility, there was an emphasis on 'keyworkers' being alongside the children immediately they anticipated a problem. They helped individual children to listen to each other and talk things through rather than to snatch or fight. Some children said how much they liked that calm yet positive approach to finding shared solutions to their conflicts. One boy compared it to another setting he used to go to where: 'it was really horrible … they all had fights and all the grown ups shouted and then they put them on the "naughty chairs" … then after … they all starts fighting again.'

When I listened to some of the adults later, I discovered that some of them had used 'naughty chairs' in their settings in the past but had found it ineffective in dealing with challenging behaviour. One child told me proudly:

When I was little I used to have to sit out there [by the big table] *on the 'naughty chair', so I leaned back … and back … and back … till it tipped over* [demonstrating] *and BANG! I fell off. I never hurt myself … everyone laughed.*

This child said he preferred the new approach in his setting, but from his nostalgic expression and clear enjoyment of his demonstration, he appeared to miss some of the excitement in his chequered past. However, the more timid children were certainly very pleased that the 'naughty chair' or 'standing in the corner' seemed to belong in the past. As one girl in that same setting told me passionately, 'if I was frightened of Miss I'd never come'. Her mother agreed that she would never leave her child with anybody who frightened children because 'she'd have nightmares and wet the bed like she used to … We couldn't stand that.'

This mother and her child were glad that there had also been a move away from a preoccupation 'with giving kids terrible nightmares by frightening them about Stranger Danger'. In most settings my identity was checked and I was usually given a special badge to let the children know that I was not a stranger to people there. I was made very welcome by them and will refer to some of the children's questions later.

Many of the children were very clear about the things they disliked about some people, I will now enlarge on those.

2(a) | Things I don't like people doing

Shouting

The few children who made negative comments about specific adults all referred to issues associated with how they dealt with challenging behaviour or discipline. They particularly disliked 'shouting'. As one of them said:

I hate people getting cross and shouting at kids. We mustn't shout, shouting's rude. Then the teachers shout [imitating adult in a very loud voice]: *'Tidy up time! Tidy up time! Stop now! Tidy up time!'*

Hurrying

As with the child in the story 'The Emperor's new clothes', Sonnyboy spoke out against the seemingly ridiculous or obvious. Once he had settled into school, he questioned his teacher about those irritating interruptions with 'why'd'you interrupt us so?' In particular, he disliked the bell and one playtime when it rang loudly in the corridor, Sonnyboy was heard grumbling, 'That don't make no sense … I just got to the interesting bit. I don't care about the time, that's plain stupid … time's as long as it takes.'

Many children talked about their intense dislike of people making them rush to tidy up or 'hurry up' at the end of sessions. In common with Sonnyboy, when they were interrupted in the middle of any enthralling activity, it caused them visible frustration or irritation. It was activities that most engaged and intrigued young children which encouraged their questions and their concentration. If they did not have to hurry it might be assumed that their learning would have been taken to a deeper level.

For most children, being stopped in the middle of that learning process was worse when little or no warning was given that a session was coming to a close. When such an interruption occurred, I observed how seldom the children were able to pick up the threads of their thinking or their action.

The fear of interruption also influenced some children in their choice of activities. A majority of settings had little spare surface or cupboard space in which unfinished puzzles or constructions could be kept. Some children said they chose never to play with certain pieces of construction equipment because they would only have to break up their models before they had time to finish them. When he talked about his favourite construction activity, one boy spoke enthusiastically about a miniature world model-making kit which involved building small wooden houses using a hammer and nails. He then added:

I never play with it up here … I never … it takes long to make all the little houses … they got real little nails … I really like it … but when I build a house it takes me a long time … and then I got to break it … tidy up time.
Another little girl in a different setting said:
All the time, it's 'Hurry up! Hurry up!' … Like in the morning, it's 'Hurry up and eat your breakfast … Hurry up, get in the car … Hurry up, we're late' … Then it's 'Hurry up … it's time' … what it time for? … packing up … I hate hurrying up.

Hurrying seemed to have become an unquestioned habit, disliked as much by the adults as by their children. The only answer to that child's question 'what it time for?' appears to be that it is always time for anything except for just being or just thinking. Adults in settings that were shared with other groups (such as those in church halls) became understandably anxious about having to pack away so much apparatus at the end of their sessions. They expressed their concern that they would 'never be able to get the children through all the Desirable Outcomes'. One child had even begun to learn Ofsted's language. She said to me: 'I can't talk now, 'cos Mum said I got to do all my de ... serious ... de ... lerious ... somefins.'

The children themselves were clearly caught up in the hurry and some felt the adults' anxiety. On a rare occasion when a child of four came into a setting in tears (there were only three among the hundred children I saw), he sat on my knee, sucked his thumb and sobbed. That day, the morning rush had been too much for him. Many children spoke to me about the way everybody had to hurry in the morning. They had a clear understanding of the complicated logistics involved in getting the children in their families to their various settings on time.

Moving to and from different situations

My research shows that, while some children aged four had boundless energy, many yawned and complained of tiredness. As one said, 'When I feel very, very tired, my teacher is kind. She pulls out the mats and lets me sleep ... lots of us have a sleep after snack time.' When I asked him whether he went to bed early he said: 'Gran gets us to bed round about eight.' He then proceeded to list all the other significant times in his day. His routine was so complicated that I needed to check the times of day he was talking about. It became clearer when I realised his hard-working mother had one all-day job and another very late at night. He competently moved the hands of a clock to the times as he spoke.

> Every day Mum picks us up from Mel [the childminder] at six [in the evening] ... then we have to catch a bus up to Gran [where he and his brother sleep from Monday to Friday]. I love it up Gran's but she got a poor old wonky leg ... Before her bad leg she picked us up herself, but now Mum has to come to Gran and fetch us in the morning at eight because she's been to work in the night ... we ain't got a dad with us no more ... then Mum takes us to Mel, then all the other kids come and we go to Playgroup. We can't have dinner there, it shuts at 12 and all the old

*people have their dinner ... Mel fetches us and we has dinner up her
house. After dinner, now I'm four, I go to another nursery ... Mel takes me
and Pete and Ali, then Mum comes to fetch me at six ... I said that
already didn't I?*

That young child was not the only one able to describe such a day
in detail. Although he commented that it made him feel tired, he did
not seem unduly concerned. His complicated routine was his normality
and he was always with people he knew well and loved. My research
disclosed that this was not true for all children. Many of them were
confused about their day. Twenty spoke in depth about the many
different childcare settings they were taken to. Their remarks
emphasised an important childcare issue and presented the children's
point of view of the demands made on young children by frequent
change.

Even when the settings for children of four were otherwise excellent,
those changes could be very demanding on them emotionally. Each
setting is bound to be different in some respects. While young
children's adaptability is fortuitous, it takes emotional robustness and
maturity to be able to relate to so many different people with differing
expectations in the same day. They also need to have good memories.
Here is one example. A girl (almost five) went in the morning to a
setting where she was given a great deal of freedom to choose activities
and to get out her equipment. In the afternoons she went to a different
place where everything was done for the children. She noticed (and
felt) the difference and described it thus:

If I could, I'd choose to stay here all day. All the people everywhere [in
each setting] *are nice, but here I plan my programme with Sally ... she's
my 'keyworker' ... all the kids plan what they will do and then we can get it*
[equipment] *all by ourself. At first, at first, I wasn't allowed at the other
place and I never knew and I got told off for helping myself to the scissors.
I remember crying ... now I know I'm not allowed. I don't know why.*

That child was very adaptable, mature and articulate. She had an
outgoing personality and, after the initial transitional difficulties, she
seemed to cope well with two settings which I was told did have very
different educational philosophies and contrasting ways of working
with the children aged four. I found many instances where children
had to contend with similar contrasts but did not cope so well.

I will now go back to one of the most significant things that the
children certainly did not like people doing – bullying.

Bullying

As remarked earlier, I found the fear of being bullied was more common than the instances of bullying itself. In some cases, older siblings had clearly warned the younger ones, 'my brother said ... bigger boys'll nick your sweets'. Many children talked negatively about playtime and said, 'I hate the playground,' even though it was not the policy of their setting to use the playground or any outdoor area while older children were there. Seldom were any children of four in any setting outside without an adult carer.

Name-calling seemed almost non-existent among the young children. The radio microphone in a reception class picked out only one such instance. In that case, a group of girls aged five took the eraser of a little girl of four on her first day at school and taunted her (under their breath) with, 'Fatty Fingers ... Fatty Fingers ... Don't let Fatty Fingers have it.'

That child was strikingly beautiful. She came from a family of large people and was much taller and plumper than the other children in the group. The older girls had spotted her difference and singled her out for their attention. The effect on her confidence was immediate. She had come into school very happily on her first morning and had not wanted her mother to stay with her. Despite the comfort and positive intervention of her teacher, she started to cry and wanted to go home. She could not settle the following day and needed her mother to stay. Tape-recordings made of her over the following two weeks showed how withdrawn and solitary she became and how much her talking diminished. In the playground she followed the teacher everywhere and implored her to 'play with me ... please play with me'.

Ten years later, while out shopping, I met and instantly recognised that same young girl. I asked her what she remembered most about starting school. Quite spontaneously she spoke about the 'horrible bully-girls who called me Fatty'. That had clouded her otherwise happy days at school. Bullying for 'being different' cannot be minimised for the effect it can have on the self-confidence and happiness of a sensitive young child. Its limited occurrence should not be exaggerated, but it must not be mistaken for the normal physical rough-and-tumble in peer-group relationships.

Just as Sonnyboy had been very distressed when he realised he had frightened some of the younger children with his stories (see p. 12), so were other children who spoke to me about being 'naughty ... you know, smacking and that'. Some of the children I observed had not yet got to grips with being in a social setting which differed from their homes. One girl, who had three older brothers, was so used to their more physical play that one push from her sent a small child flying. The child was too shocked even to cry, but the girl who had pushed was very tearful. It would have been possible for anyone who had not been watching closely to assume that the girl was a potential bully. No such assumption was made and she was given the comfort and sensitive support she needed by an adult while some of the children cuddled the little child who had been knocked over. He then started to cry because he was being squeezed too hard.

When sufficient time was taken to listen to the children and watch them at play, the adults remarked how much easier it was to anticipate conflict or to spot any potential bullying.

Unlike the children whose early days had been clouded by fears, a majority of the children described their favourite thing as 'playing with friends'.

3 | Playing with friends and having fun

Some of the quieter children appeared to gain pleasure simply from being with each other, smiling contentedly with arms entwined. More outgoing, exuberant children told me how much they loved being with their friends and one pair added 'we love laughing and laughing'. To show what they meant, they rolled on the ground, giggling helplessly. Some gave details of their favourite games, complete with appropriate sound effects.

Freedom to explore
Those who had free use of an outside area often talked imaginatively with me about 'being adventurous ... playing in the jungle ... well, not really ... it's only pretend ... climbing high up and jumping off ... Wheeee! that's *really* scary.'

Many of the children expressed the belief that they were there to play with friends. One young child spoke enthusiastically about how he 'loves to play in the garden with friends ... to explore outside, climb and jump ... swing ... ride the bikes ... GREAT!'

In their own way, many more children complained bitterly about how few opportunities and how little time they had to be physical in their settings. They were able to explain that very well, perhaps because it had real meaning for them. They loved chasing and hiding but many complained that they 'can only go outside sometimes ... teacher must come ... gotta be safe'.

The need to protect young children and keep them safe from harm, yet allow them to take risks, seems to have become a problem for adults and some children. In my research, there were certainly few opportunities for children to be independent in making their own choices or being independent of adult supervision or control. They had to remain within sight of the staff.

When he was six, one of my grandsons talked with me about some of the concerns with regard to keeping children safe. He remembered being a young infant living in the countryside where had had enjoyed much freedom and, by four, was 'playing with my friends out of doors in Sue's wonderful nursery! I loved Sue.'

By six, he was a very independent and self-reliant child. When he spoke to me he was feeling very cross because he was not allowed to play in the park by himself, he told me:

> Jacqui-Nan, I feel really fed up! Everyone wants their kids to be independent and to grow up, grow up, don't be a baby ... It's like that with cuddlies. Then it's not like it when you want to go to the park on your own to play! Then you're not allowed because it's too dangerous. You get murdered and that. Where can we go to play and be independent?

In a recent survey of 200 parents in Manchester, Glasgow, Bristol and London, 85% said they were so affected by concerns about their children's safety that their fears impaired their quality of life.[20] Their fear of strangers attacking their children was greater than their fear of traffic, despite statistical evidence that the latter presented far greater risks. Yet remaining closeted at home could deprive them of the very strategies which they need to keep safe. There must be a balance.

For more practical help with giving children their freedom and helping them build their lifeskills in a safe but not over-managed environment, see Jennie Lindon's *Too safe for their own good?*[21]

Playing outside

A lack of independence to explore can seriously affect young children's learning and their development in many ways. As so many of the children in my study implied, playing out of doors is one of the most pleasurable ways to make friends. Self-confidence is gained as children learn to judge their physical limits and persevere to extend those limits by challenging and testing themselves.

Many children whom I observed to be developing well needed more time to practise activities. Few had the same opportunities as the following little boy with poor physical coordination. He tried repeatedly (for almost 17 minutes) to gain the courage to climb the

---

20 Jenkins, T. (1998) 'Families for freedom', paper given at a Barnardo conference.
21 Lindon, J. (1999) *Too safe for their own good?*, National Early Years Network.

ladder of a slide and then slide down. At each attempt he got a little further up the rungs and then climbed down. When he finally climbed to the top and teetered there, everyone watching held their breath. When he slid down to the bottom everyone spontaneously cheered. Then, without a moment's hesitation, he climbed up again and slid down. He did it again and again. It was a developmental milestone in his young life and he could barely wait to show his mother what he could do when she came to collect him. The whole ethos of that setting was celebratory and encouraged him to be persistent. As one practitioner said: 'It's who they are as people that counts more than any outcomes they achieve. The young ones need to know they're all special, all good at something.'

When children went to two different settings, one in the morning and another in the afternoon, they were sometimes able to make comparisons between them. Invariably they chose as their favourite the setting with a garden, especially if they were free to go outside to explore or play. Many settings that did not have sole use of an outside area frequently only had a corner of a car park next to a busy road. That was as common in rural settings as in inner cities. Few opportunities were apparent for those children to be independent or to make their own choice to be out of doors. Even in those setting that had more outdoor space, there were few opportunities for children of four to dig in soil unaided or to explore the outside environment with friends or for long periods.

For most four year olds, to 'go outside' involved going out all together with their educators. Only in a few smaller settings did some young children have gardens for their pleasure and free exploration. In those, there were small sets of gardening tools for the children's own use and animals to look after, including hens which gave daily eggs. Children who lived in high-rise flats or bed and breakfast accommodation often had to wait for babies to be fed before being taken for a walk or 'to the play park'. One of these children told me that if he could choose anything in the world it would be:

A garden. I would love a garden and watching butterflies and digging vegetables. Me and my friends love learning about all the little creatures and all that … In the night I dream about a house for my mum and a garden with a big tree for me and my friends to climb.

In all the settings, the children said how much they loved being allowed to play on their tricycles and tractors. Some took many risks and showed great skill in their driving. Many girls as well as boys spoke about wheeled toys as their favourite things. When there were adequate large resources to share comfortably, there was little tension or quarrelling among the children. Where resources were inadequate, the children became impatient about 'waiting turns' and were tearful and fractious.

'Dressing up' outside was also described as 'great fun'. Settings with a secure commitment to imaginative play made role play a particular priority in their indoor and outdoor environments. Some role play I observed was relaxed, imaginative and prolonged, with the children taking the lead in elaborately conceived plots based on real and imaginary situations. Many of their educators supported them by, for example, providing an old trunk with dressing-up clothes and bedspreads to make dens. They also became involved themselves, and a flamboyant little girl of four (who was an articulate character like Sonnyboy) announced:

> When I's big I's going to be a big, big star ... a pop star, yeah! A big 'Afro-Spice' ... Best of all I love making up dancing bits and then Miss plays on a drum ... Boom! Ta ta boom! [singing]: 'We can play on the big bass drum' ... and this the way she do it ... Boom! I loves teacher. She lets me pretend all I like.

In some of the larger settings there was less role play outside, but the older children frequently said they enjoyed playing cooperative traditional games such as 'Oranges and lemons' or others which involved singing, clapping and skipping. Some of the younger children liked to watch but not to join in.

Sadly, many children aged four whom I observed to be healthily noisy and noticeably active in their settings were in cramped and crowded conditions with very little space indoors or out to spontaneously 'let off steam' or play in an essentially physical way. It came to light in discussion with staff that many of those same children also lived in bed and breakfast accommodation or crowded flats and were not allowed to make either a mess or a noise at home. In conversation with the children one said he felt 'fed up of keeping quiet'. It is salutary to consider that such continual restriction of young adults in a prison would be likely to result in an enquiry and action by the authorities. Although children in these settings were not actually tied down it must have felt like that to them, with all their natural physical and emotional energy bursting to come out. Many aspects of their normal development would be impaired but all those children could do was complain: 'We can't play nowhere ... we got nowhere to play.' That plea to play should be a matter of real concern to everybody in society.

When I continued to listen to another group of children in a rural area it was clear that they, too, needed to be able to play much more frequently with their friends in their setting. One told me with great enthusiasm about the special times when teacher put the climbing frame outside. That was his (and his friends') favourite time, but the various pieces of large apparatus were not used on a regular basis because the cupboard was across a yard and the frame was very heavy to carry. As one very energetic child said:

> If I could choose what to do every day, I'd practise climbing higher and higher up the big frame ... and football, yeah ... football every day ... shooting gold! Gold! My big brother's good at football ... he got a cup for scoring golds.

4 | Cooking food and feasting together

Snack time, and especially 'having picnics' or 'having dinner all together' was a favourite event for the children in most settings. Relaxed conversations and happy social interaction abounded.

Creative snack time

Eating time was used by some adults to extend literacy, either with songs or rhymes about food or with stories about special events such as birthdays. They also encouraged the children to recognise their names by putting the children's name cards on different chairs (or cushions) each day and getting them to find their places. The adults stood by to help and I was told by the majority of children that this snack-time activity was 'like a party game ... it's fun'.

Children who could not find their place told me they enjoyed playing the game 'hunt your place'. It was touching to see how many children helped each other. In his excitement, one child in a wheelchair spun his chair round so fast that he knocked many cards on to the floor. He and his friends laughed and a new game emerged in which he played 'teacher' and whizzed round the table rearranging the cards where he wanted his friends to sit. Watchful support by sensitive adults was a key to such total enjoyment. The children who took part certainly did not become confused or anxious, and the more able took pleasure in recognising their own names and those of some of their friends.

I noticed later that some of them spontaneously tried to write those names during role play when they held 'pretend parties'. Independently, they found name cards to copy and wrote invitations or place cards for the table. These were often elaborately decorated with numbers and patterns around the edge. Some children remembered how to write their names and those of their special friends without looking at the cards. As they wrote, they frequently named each letter and made up their own rhymes and songs. That pleasurable sharing of food and the imaginative activities which spontaneously evolved was obviously beneficial to the whole development of the children.

By contrast, snack time was more formally organised in some settings. It was used during a half-hour session of 'large group' to teach the alphabet and phonics, days of the week and numbers chanted from a chart. In those settings at 'snack time' there was little spontaneous conversation or activity. When I analysed the quality of learning I found that half hour to be of minimal value because many children did not speak and had 'switched off'. As one child described it to me: 'This is the most boring thing in my whole day.'

Cooking

The next most popular event for the children centred on 'cooking'. In most settings, each child was able to weigh out or measure their own ingredients rather than have an adult do it all and then pass round a large bowl for them to stir. 'Do it meself, do it meself!' was a frequent plea. There were many adults who let the children help with weighing but justified using only one bowl. They gave as their reasons: expense, waste of ingredients, and the need for children to work cooperatively and to share. Surprisingly, many children loved savoury foods and baking 'cheesy biscuits and eating veggie thingies, like carrots'.

Once again, many children enjoyed the opportunity to link activities such as cooking to games which encouraged exploration through the senses. Many talked about their 'tasting and smelly games' and in a few settings some children were confident enough to test my capability in recognising some of the different items. At times like that, I found the children asked the most searching questions. Their curiosity about all manner of things was aroused by those practical activities when they took the initiative. I will be returning to that subject when some of the children's spontaneous conversations are explored (see pp. 47–50).

I found another a marvellous example of a young child taking the initiative in a different setting. He told me he had spent hours during that term with a friend cutting out pictures of various foods from magazines. They were also collecting labels of foodstuffs to make their own scrap book. That child told me he would 'go to the shop with Dad to buy some of them [pointing to pictures of fruit] and put them on the science table ... I made a book before and Miss put it there.'

At four years and eight months, this child had already begun to select those foods that grew in his geographical area and those which came from abroad to make a 'big picture chart for the wall'. When I asked him how he had managed all this work, he told me that nobody had set him that problem, he had done it 'all by myself' and his friend had joined in. It was particularly interesting when the staff in his setting remarked:

> We just make sure Joe has a box to put his book and his collections. He's a bright little lad ... believe it or not he didn't used to be confident ... a simple thing like that has helped him and some of the others join in when they see what he does. The practical side really did pay off. He's so proud of himself.

5 | Finding out about different people

In those areas of Britain with few people from minority ethnic groups, the children told me about other even more exciting activities which they enjoyed, especially the 'very interesting visitors' who came to their settings. Photographs of those visitors and the past events they had taken part in with them sparked many long conversations. They recalled many details of the foods and colourful artefacts they had brought with them. As one child explained to me: 'Them's got Nannas and Grandpas from Africa and a long way off in Jamaica but them all born in a big city like Birmingham. Wish they was here all days.'

Some of those visitors from other cultures combined the arts (poetry, art, music and dance) with the sharing of more exotic fruits and vegetables. Those real events led to shared feasts, festivals and mini carnivals. Rural children who had little experience of people from other cultures said they found those experiences 'real fun', especially when they joined in 'drumming and dancing'.

Those were often the most creative times I observed in any settings, and the richest in terms of the quality of the children's learning. The children listened enthralled to storytellers and musicians, then joined them to freely express themselves either in dance, making masks, beating rhythms, making puppets or telling stories.

In some settings, arts events for young children had always played a big part in the curriculum and often lasted for a week. Because I had missed the actual event, the children shared everything with me when I visited. One group was very imaginative and wanted to take me for an adventure on their 'magic carpet'. A boy took me by the hand and led me outside announcing to other children in his most magic voice:

> Come, come to the magic lands on my magic carpet ... We love the magic carpet! We been to Africa, to desert lands. We found lots of different

people. Come on my magic carpet ... magic lands ... real people ... camels ... magic lands.

As I sat on a log in their garden (transformed by the children into 'a throne for the queen'), I listened to them as they created their other world. On that particular day we were being transported to space. It became their idea of 'heaven ... high up in heaven ... high in the starry sky'. Everything they touched was transformed; rough stones became 'precious pearls for the necklace of the angels', dingy brown leaves turned into 'tiny jewelled plates to catch the stardust. Stardust is very, very magic. It makes sick children better. Catch it! Catch it! Get the magic net, get the magic net.' Another boy lifted up the branches of a bush – that had become his magic net. His face was serious in case he missed that stardust. He caught it. They cheered, then sang as they sprinkled it around: 'Sprinkle sprinkle stardust bright, make the children well tonight.' I wished I had had a video to record the magical moments of those children.

It was very clear that those multicultural arts events had encouraged creativity by nurturing the children's imaginations. Their educators told me that the children had made their own recordings of various sound effects to go with their magic carpet. They had also asked their visitors many pertinent questions about their families and their different ways of life. Finding out so much about other people had extended the children in every possible way. The children told me that when their visitors left, they took their own magic carpet with them. Some children had cried and wanted to go with them. One child who loved their lively music wondered whether 'up in London, they party all the time?'

In my research, I found the encouragement of young children's imagination and creativity had been sorely neglected. It showed in the fact that very few children chose artistic activities as their favourites. The apparent marginalisation of the arts is another crucial issue to which I return later (see pp. 60–65).

6 | Finding out about all sorts of things

It was unclear whether the children chose this as a favourite activity because they enjoyed the actual process of 'finding out about all sorts of things' or whether their pleasure was more associated with the feeling of confidence in being free to make their own choices and doing things independently. 'I did it by myself!' was a frequent boast, accompanied by beaming smiles which reflected the children's greatest pleasure.

The girls in particular were more specific and referred frequently to 'feeling very happy and more grown up' when left to find out or to experiment by themselves. In the settings where equality of opportunity was working well, it was the girls who chose to spend more time than the boys on setting up and using the computer and the tape-recorder. In one of the settings that included much younger children, I watched a tiny girl of two years ten months show another girl of four how to control 'mousie' and play a complex mathematical matching game which relied for success on manipulative skills and memory. As a child under three, she was so quick that she followed visual instructions to change the program to more and more challenging games on similar themes. The other child found it difficult to keep up with her. That episode only lasted a matter of eight minutes and then the other child was able to have her turn. She too became very skilled in controlling the mouse but said she saw little point in playing games: 'It's alright but it's pretty boring sitting there. I like finding out *real* things.'

She went to the discovery table to look at some flowers through a magnifying glass.

Some other girls in the same setting said they did not like playing with the mechanical or pre-programmed toys. One turned to me and explained why: 'That's boys stuff! War and all that, I hates it. Boys always make guns.' Though many of those toys did not have a particularly militaristic appearance, the boys observed did use them in that way. They also used the outdoor area as a combat zone and said: [*pointing a stick to shoot me*] 'Our favourite thing's playing war.'

Fabulous creepy crawlies

When I listened to children in settings with a garden or where adults took them for walks, all the children appeared curious about plants and living creatures – all except one, that is, who said to me: 'Yuk! I hates worms and slimey snails and spiders … spiders are the end!' But another spoke for the majority when he said, 'I especially liked finding snails and worms outside', though he seldom had the opportunity 'because we stops in most days … I don't know why … I love outside best.'

The children's favourite event in many settings was their 'teddy bears' picnic in the woods'. From the photographs, some of those woods had little more than half a dozen trees but as one child described: 'I saw millions of woodlices. I love crawly woodlices.' In other settings there were few indoor areas of discovery or 'interest tables'. The learning potential of those was obviously underestimated, being seen by staff as 'yet another thing to be tidied away'. Those where I positioned myself to watch and listen to the children had a selection of living and found objects for children to puzzle over, such as the mechanism of an old sewing machine. The concentration span of the children seemed to extend according to the level of curiosity such things encouraged.

I was frequently shown the magnifying glass and bug boxes, and the children appeared willing and able to take care of mini beasts and other animals on a regular basis. One child told me he found the worms in their wormery the best things to watch because they were 'very interesting creatures … they burrow underground, did you know that?' He went on to tell me that he preferred ants and asked me whether I also knew that 'ants are tiny, tiny civilisations. Like the Romans, they march across the land and they have lots of slaves. I saw that on television a long time ago … interesting.'

Like that child, many other children of four showed a degree of sophistication in their knowledge and seriously discussed 'finding out how creatures live'. Another child talked to me about the various investigative activities she had taken part in already in her setting using 'bug boxes, magnets and … my favourite things … magnifying glasses to make insects (and eyes) look bigger. My favourite things are science.'

Fabulous science

'MAGNIFYING GLASSES!' were identified as the most popular piece of equipment by a majority of the children. It was quite common for me to see young children peering at the enlarged eye of a friend who was trying to focus on a specimen. Some children asked questions and managed to work out how our eyes work. For example, a boy of four years and eight months noticed 'a black dot thingy going in and out … look … that black dot [laughing and getting closer] … a round circle … look it's bigger … great big eye thingy … It a hole?'

That was a profoundly scientific observation that sprang from a puzzling and enjoyable starting point of investigation by the child. His observations showed that he could see the mechanics of the eye in terms of the working of the iris and the pupil. He knew that a circle is round. 'It a hole?' was a very accurate guess about the pupil. In his case, the discovery went unnoticed because the adult was too far away to hear. She called out: 'Stop messing about you boys. Come here and get on with your work!' At that time the work was dull by comparison – colouring in a printed picture of ladybirds, counting their spots and writing a line of letter Ls. They complied but, tutting loudly, one boy said 'I hates this silly work. *[He saw me watching and explained]* I only like finding out things.'

7 | Beautiful books, stories and learning to read and write

A storyteller in the family

Sonnyboy's family nickname was very apt. His sunny personality and flashing smile shone through the gloom of the winter's day when my research began. He had expressive blue eyes and his extravagant gestures gave him a presence as a young storyteller. He had been born into a traditionally oral culture which, for generations, had depended more upon their talking than reading. It is of interest in our multicultural society that their families' first language for the past three generations was English with a strong southern Irish dialect.

Sonnyboy had an insatiable curiosity and his questions were often challenging, but tempered with a natural warmth and gentleness. His mother described him as:

'Lovable ... very lively and talkative ... kind ... deep thinkin' and sensitive. From the age of three ... always telling stories to the little 'uns.'

'Come and look at our beautiful books!' was a common invitation proffered to me by many children of four. Beautiful books and stories were very high on the list of their favourite activities. Most of the children spoke warmly about the stories they had at home at bedtime. My research has shown that those traditions of bedtime stories have certainly not been entirely lost. Many of the children were able to tell me their own favourite traditional stories – 'The three bears' was the most popular. Children who told those stories used all the different voices and actions, and some of them had similar storytelling abilities to Sonnyboy, but none was as dramatic or fluent. In various settings, some were able to catch the attention of younger children, draw them together to listen and catch their interest, sometimes using puppets or other props kept with the storybooks.

One of the children's greatest dislikes was 'being squashed all together for storytime, everyone wriggling and all that'.

Many children of four came to me and offered to 'read you a story'. As they did so, I was able to watch how well the children pointed to words, followed the print left to right, recognised letters of their names and turned the pages as they repeated their own versions. All that awareness of print pointed to their understanding of the reading process. At that early stage they impose their own meaning upon print. Book illustrations help them to do that and in my observations they were very important to most children, particularly those which related to real life or were humorous. Letterbox Library – a cooperative which supplies quality multicultural, non-sexist and special interest titles for children and people who work with them – was mentioned by many children, especially among African-Caribbean children.[22] In some settings they had a special 'Letterbox' shelf containing many familiar tales from other cultures. I could hear children laughing at those books which challenged stereotyping or gender bias, such as Prince Cinders. Some children said they asked their teacher for the same funny stories and she read them again and again. They thoroughly enjoyed sharing 'BIG, BIG STORYBOOKS!'

Beginning to read

While the younger children and those less mature were content to look at books and listen to stories, many of the more mature and confident children were highly motivated and enthusiastic about becoming readers. Some read very fluently already. I made a particular point of asking their families how they had achieved that feat so young. It was noticeable that in every case the families said their children had 'caught' reading rather than being 'taught' by them using any specific methods. How their children had learnt to read was a mystery to them. Most emphasised that they were keen readers themselves and had always read their children lots of stories. One mother of a child who was reading fluently by herself at four elaborated:

> She taught herself. She was always curious about words on packets and in her books. In the car she began to read the signs … she kept asking what the words said. Suddenly one day I realised she was reading her storybook.

That mother was very quick to point out that she had done exactly the same for her other children with little or no effect. One sibling had taken until the age of six to show any real interest. Other families agreed about such differences between their children and another told me that one of her daughters had taken until eight and a half to begin to read fluently, despite every encouragement. With hindsight, she questioned whether it might have been better to wait because she had noticed that, at around the age of seven, the child began to compare herself so unfavourably with her friends and became quite depressed

---

22 Letterbox Library, *Celebrating equality and diversity in the best children's books*, tel 020 7226 1633; fax 020 7226 1768.

because she always tried so hard and could not crack it. Her mother thought that spending so much time:

> trying so hard meant she simply wasn't ready. Her brain ... something hadn't developed yet ... I don't know how to explain it, but I think keeping on going over and over it like I did with her was stupid. I wasn't worried really, but she got very uptight. She reads perfectly now ... it suddenly clicked with her.

That mother's positive attitudes contrasted with those in other settings where there was a lot of pressure and anxiety on the part of the children and adults about reading. In the whole of my research, that was the only time I ever saw some children of four become very agitated. Others who were quite confident became very competitive, as they compared the books they were on with each other. Just before they were five, most children took 'reading books' home but it had not been clearly understood by either the children or their families that some of those books did not tell any particular story, they were simply to be 'talked about' together. The mothers sometimes brought tearful children into the settings to apologise because they did not 'manage to learn all the words'.

Prior to that, the children had not been afraid of any of the adults, yet to 'fail' so young as a reader was having a profound effect on their feelings about themselves and the staff. Even children who had expressed the most enthusiasm for books did not mention enjoying their 'reading' books. Some of the children and their families had underestimated how slow that reading process can be and seemed disappointed not to succeed immediately.

I found that many librarians helped people relax about reading and to enjoy it more. In inner city areas, good use was made by many settings of the local library, particularly for factual books of information. The rural children occasionally had visits from mobile book and toy libraries so that they, too, could borrow books. However, while the contents of those mobiles was the same as in the local libraries, they had sometimes been more roughly handled and even the young children remarked that they 'didn't like tatty books'.

Some librarians linked closely with their nearby settings and visited them to read stories. Frequently these were new editions out of the financial reach of the settings. When it was practically possible, these librarians welcomed whole groups of children into the library for stories or to choose books each week. As one child said: 'That is my very favourite thing. Library time's a very special treat. We goes up the library Friday. I got a ticket for my own book ... Mum's got one for Joel (the baby). We love it up the library.'

A number of children also said how much they 'love singing rhymes', some adding: 'We do that in group time ... That's my favourite.' They seemed to enjoy the predictability of some of those and enjoyed joining in. In the summer, many children like this girl said: 'My very favourite thing is to bring a nice book outside to look at with my friend.' Those children were amongst the most fortunate and had a tree or an awning to sit under to share a book or as another girl said to me 'we enjoys a good natter in the sun'. She raised a very interesting point there.

The need to 'natter'
Talking or using oral language was not educationally valued and was most commonly dismissed by the adults as 'nattering or chattering'. In most settings the talk of children was seriously underestimated as a tool for thinking. As I have written already, most of the talking consisted of adults asking questions. But I found it was in spontaneous and prolonged conversations and discussions between the children that I found most examples of the children's puzzling minds. Often, the children were interrupted before they had had a chance to finish what they were saying or working through their thoughts and ideas. There were many things they needed to talk through, such as working through a sequence in a game or following a construction pattern. The children themselves picked up the habit of butting in. When I was listening to a child telling me about the metamorphosis of a butterfly, a younger child interrupted him and said to me: 'He's big now ... got to get on with his proper work.' After that, I noticed how many other children interrupted each other in the middle of similar discussions. Talking was not treated as proper work and some children had serious reservations about talking as well as about playing.

A majority of children said they 'love to play ... but...' and then qualified their enjoyment with a comment similar to this: 'Now I'm four, I come to nursery (playgroup, school) to learn me to read and write.' Playing and 'school' work such as reading and writing were separated by adults and therefore also by children. I heard many call to children engaged in conversations to 'come along now and get on with your work'. The children's expectations of work was having to sit at their tables to do writing, usually either copying from cards or worksheets with alphabetical letters or phonics or numerals to ten. When they had finished their more formal tasks, many children chose to draw or make writing patterns, and some – like Sonnyboy – wrote their own stories in what he called 'my own scribble writing'.

Beginning to write

As adults we often see scribble or scribbling as a waste of time; we believe it to be meaningless. It is not. In this context, 'scribble writing' is the children's own emerging script. It begins in early infancy as babies draw in their custard (or whatever else they manage to spill) on the tray in front of them. From those accidental beginnings, mark-making develops as a young child's way of imposing their own meaning or their own personal construction of their world. By the time they are four they are using their mark-making to communicate messages for others and become more aware of its connection with our writing. A number of children pointed to certain parts of their script and said: 'This is the grown-up bits ... look ... DDD ... D for Debbie. I'm Debbie and ... r r r ... I can write r ... I can write grown-up things and my own stories. Read this now.'

Debbie gave it to me to read, assuming that I would understand every word. Many children in so many settings showed me their own emerging writing with similar pride. Of course, some of it was difficult for me to read. I am an adult and I could not possibly impose the same meanings on what they had written. It was an intrinsic part of their own world. When I asked them if they would read it for me they did so enthusiastically. I noticed how their voice inflections changed, for example when the writing was a telephone message or represented a shopping list which, by the way, was written down a page. So much learning about writing was embedded in what they did and what they said.

Those settings with specific role play areas for things such as shopping, the office, hospital or a travel agency had paper and pencils, diaries, maps, timetables and appointment books. The children enjoyed making and using their own telephone directory and wrote lists and messages in their own emergent writing. In many cases, families and other educators had not heard of emergent or developmental writing. They became fascinated when I discussed it with them and they examined their children's writing more closely. They, too, recognised some of the letters which resembled letters from the children's experiences or culture. Similarly, they were amazed at the ability of their children to recognise, to write numerals and to solve problems of addition, subtraction and sharing in the course of their play.

There was a common underestimation of the value of play activities for literacy and numeracy development. Role play areas were invariable seen as means for children's 'socialisation'. In their anxiety to achieve end-products, even the staff in settings with exciting and stimulating role play areas did not fully recognise their learning potential and that they should be included in their specific plans. They frequently interrupted the free flow of the children's imaginative play. They were unaware that they (the adults) were encouraging, through their provision, some of the richest experiences for the consolidation and extension of literacy and numeracy.

In other settings, where there was even less experience or understanding of the potential of role play, those areas were so poorly planned and resourced it became clear that they were only there because someone thought they ought to be. Many did not know why. The areas were left virtually unattended and certainly unobserved. The play in them provided few opportunities for any rich or stimulating learning. Consequently, the play frequently disintegrated and the whole situation became time-wasting and chaotic. In some cases it was a very frightening space for the more timid children and they did not enjoy areas like that. One boy told me: 'No, I never go there ... I think it's about dressing up or something. No that's a waste of time! Horrible! All shouting and that ... horrible ... I'm not frightened.'

I was very frightened. The children had begun to throw the pretend food and pans in my direction and I was relieved when somebody else noticed and play was stopped. Like that child, I found it all an absolute waste of the children's time. The whole point of play as the work of young children had been missed. Many educators said they felt inept in their organisation and management of play.

Many children of four told me how much they liked some of the set routines in their settings. A majority had time set aside for them at each session for phonics and copy writing. When that formal time of 'playing at school!' was limited to 20 minutes, with five minutes or less for 'doing my very best writing', I noticed that the children took great care and appeared very content as they coloured in their worksheets. I also noticed that, without an adult alongside, a majority formed their letters incorrectly. Some of their formations were imaginative but incorrect and confusing. I was dubious about whether poor letter formation would be easy to correct later because the brain was 'learning' some very bizarre patterning. Beyond five minutes of concentrated effort, pencils were clutched by tense fingers and worried frowns appeared on children's faces; they began to wriggle and complain about their aching hands and shoulders.

My research certainly showed that the vast majority of children aged four in every setting was doing well in the area of literacy. What was even more important: apart from very few exceptions, they were enjoying the process of becoming readers and writers. They said so, and their enthusiasm was apparent. Many adults in their settings were doing a magnificent job but needed much more training, specifically in child development and its relevance to their provision and observation of role play. That would help them to identify the young children's strengths and struggles with greater accuracy and to recognise the golden opportunities for learning which they were now missing. To be able to plan more developmentally appropriate ways for the children to meet curriculum requirements can be a creative and powerful experience, powerful enough to give all educators the confidence to insist that unhealthy and damaging pressure is taken off our young children. Perhaps without that stress, even in our secondary schools, everyone might be invited to 'come and look at our beautiful books!'.

I believe as a society, we have a chance to make that happen. The 1999 National Year of Reading focused on reading partnerships with families, and books of increasingly high quality now find their way on to many more shelves. It all seems very promising but I hope it does not backfire and result in even more pressure on young children to read before they are really ready. Switching off young children to reading is going to be a very hard pattern to change, but when I listened to children talk on the theme of mathematics, it seems doubtful that we ever switch them on for very long.

8 | Playing shops, building with bricks and making patterns and shapes

In one setting a boy of four looked over my shoulder as I turned the page of my notebook. He pointed to a word in large print and asked, 'What does that say?'. I read it to him, 'MATHEMATICS'. He laughed. 'What's maf-e-ma-ticks? ... ticks an' that?' Before I had time to answer another child joined in:

> Yeah! You get ticks ... writing numbers and counting and stuff like that ... and doing sums ... and getting lots of ticks. I love ticks ... Like when you count all them little spots, you got to colour all the little shapes then you put a number then that's a sum, then sums get hard and more hard and no one can do them, that's what my brother says. He tells me, 'You wait till you get to big school'. I won't like sums when I can't do them, will I? I won't get ticks up big school.

I will return shortly to that issue about 'big school' (see pp. 59–60), but remain briefly with the children's connection between maths and ticks. In most settings, doing sums and getting ticks seemed very important to a few children, but even more so to the adults around them, whether family or staff. They were seen by families as a sign that their children were doing well and by the staff as a sign of their own success.

Sums were not mentioned by the children as their favourite activities, but playing mathematically certainly was. Many children made very positive comments like the following child about such play:

> I love playing shops and all that … like building and making all the different shapes. I like cutting out all the pictures and I write numbers … 1, 2, 3, 4, 5 … I can count more than 100 … and a million is big … like the stars.

In their play, a majority of children were able to name each shape and some were very imaginative in using them. In all those cases, their thinking had been taken further because they were able to experiment more. I saw one particularly demanding example of that when two children were tiling a doll's-house floor. They had been challenged by the adult to make sure they left no gaps in the middle. They spent most of their morning session absorbed in that task and had developed some regular patterns as they worked. One of them reported to me:

> I enjoyed doing that a lot. Can you see we made those patterns at the edge? They are red, white, red, white … then we ran out and did green, yellow, green, yellow. We've just had the kitchen tiled at home and Dad had to cut some tiles because they wouldn't fit. He said one of the walls wasn't square. I don't know what that means … the wall looks like a rectangle … like that wall over there. That's not a square, is it?

If she had been nearby, it would have been interesting to see how that question might have been answered by the child's imaginative keyworker, who had allowed those children so much time to play mathematically. I also noted how many other curriculum areas such as language, creative, social and physical development were well covered by that activity.

Role play and 'real money'

I observed the children using mathematics with pleasure and sustained concentration in many role play areas. On these occasions, they were trying to solve some of the most challenging mathematical problems and gain a deeper understanding of very complex mathematical concepts. It was inspiring to watch two young children using the scales and arguing with an older brother in Postman Pat's Post Office that the smallest parcel was the heaviest and would therefore cost more to send. In another small shop (while all his friends nodded) one told me:

This is my favourite place to play and we can even dress up. I specially like all the real things on the shelves [packets of food]. *We've got proper weighing scales and we've got a little till for the money ... sometimes we have real money. Look!*

Sonnyboy would have been pleased; he so disliked plastic coins. 'What's these plastic bits you're giving me?' he once asked his teacher. Many of the other children disliked them too. In one setting, where everything had to be packed away by midday, I watched two children on their hastily improvised market stall. They were arguing with each other furiously about the price of a packet of tea. One of them had little idea of realistic prices as she wrote on the small chalkboard she set up for the day. The other child, a prospective customer, was more worldly wise and made it plain to her friend that she was not going to pay. She screeched at her: 'What! £3 for a packet of tea! That's ridiculous. Look, it even says one pound and 30 pee on the other label. I'm not giving you £3, no way! I'd pay £1 ... that's it.'

Those same girls had already told me how much they enjoyed playing. 'We love pretending but especially when we got all real things, like real money and we can count it all ... and then Miss helps. You can help as well if you want.'

Checking real money back into the till and matching all the coins was a demanding task, but some children were able to do it competently. To include 'real things' in their play must have been significant to the children because so many showed them to me when they talked about their favourite things. I observed that many children had 'real telephones'. One child told me very proudly how they had made a phone book of their own:

Our own little directory ... we went round and asked everyone their number, then we wrote them all in a book and we put 'Telephone Directory' on the cover. I done that by myself ... I copied it off that one [pointing to a local directory]. *I especially like doing things by myself ... I mean with my friends, but ... you know ... choosing and then just getting on ... playing and all that.*

That setting had a mobile phone and the staff gave the children one turn each week to use it, as one child told me:

To phone a real person ... I'll phone my nanna! I'll say, 'Hello Nanna, it's me ... How are you?' And she'll say, 'Hello my little sweetheart', 'cos that's what she always calls me ... I love phoning Nanna, but I musn't talk long it's too expensive ... That's what my mum tells my brother. He's always nattering on the phone ... football stuff.

Many children were already aware of the price of telephoning; it was part of their own lives. In one setting I listened as two girls argued about a television advertisement which told everyone how cheap it was to make calls. 'Absolute rubbish!' said one child. 'It is so! ... it's cheaper if you phone at night,' her friend snapped.

To add even more realism to their role play, some of the staff had made various administrative forms for passport applications, licences, pensions and benefits which customers (including staff) had to complete. Those particular children were already familiar with 'form filling' in their lives. Clearly, their staff saw the mathematical value in what they were doing for the children by providing them with meaningful mathematical experiences. For the children, it was those realistic yet imaginative activities which enabled them to impose their own interpretations and meanings on their many worlds. With gusto and little understanding, they also sang their two times table. Why? One of the adults explained: 'Well it doesn't do any harm, and keeps their families happy.'

Some settings linked mathematics to their stories and events such as those mentioned earlier about the 'magic carpet' (pp. 46–47). In that case mathematics was linked creatively to printed patterns and symmetry which occur in nature. One child was very excited to show me 'my very own magic carpet its a tiny little one for my doll ... like it?'

Miniature world play and mathematics were very popular, and the children combined that frequently with construction toys and large block play. It was of particular interest to observe how well most of the children were able to manage addition, subtraction, sharing and simple fractions in those play situations but how confused they became when the staff translated the same problems into a written form or worksheets of sums. That appears to confirm the findings of Martin Hughes.[23] In his experiments in addition and subtraction, he found that when young children used 'real' objects they could make very complex calculations. Yet many of those same children (some much older than four) experienced difficulties in transferring what they knew in real and meaningful situations to understanding abstract symbolisation, such as in sums. It was being forced to make that transfer or change to abstraction too soon which appeared to create the greatest confusion and anxiety for the children.

Adult fear of maths
A majority of the adults in a wide variety of settings expressed their own anxiety about mathematics. Many did not recognise the mathematical

---

23 Hughes, M. (1986) *Children and number: difficulties in learning mathematics*, Blackwells.

LIVERPOOL JOHN MOORES UNIVERSITY
LEARNING SERVICES

possibilities in the excellent role play areas which they had set up so laboriously for their children. In the main, staff gave 'the children's socialising' as their main purpose for setting up those play activities.

In some settings, they urged me to examine all the children's sum books. I did so, but it was difficult to reassure the staff that, in their play, the children had achieved all Ofsted's requirements; further, that they were being challenged to think much more deeply. Most importantly, in a subject in which an entire nation appears to be failing, they were thoroughly enjoying mathematics and had told me so.

There was an almost total lack of training in this crucial area. Unlike their children, staff and families alike told me how much that they had 'hated maths at school ... I haven't got a clue how to teach it to the little ones.' For them 'big school' was certainly where they did not get any ticks and where they constantly faced their own sense of failure. I believe that, as a result of feeling so insecure, only a limited number of staff felt confident enough to trust their instincts about the importance of play and to fully recognise the mathematical value of many of the excellent play activities which they were already providing. It was those which a majority of the children had chosen as their favourites so enthusiastically; but in their comments, as we talked about maths, they were already saying: 'No, I can't like that!' Had some of the older children's and the adults' fears already rubbed off?

I found in my research, particularly in the area of mathematics, that being prepared for 'big school' meant they were not being considered in the here and now. To find so many young children unprepared to risk making mistakes or afraid of mathematics so young is of very serious concern to any educator. We must retain young children's natural fascination and sparkle which we are in danger of dousing. Play with such a positive purpose was being consistently misunderstood and misinterpreted.

9 | Painting, collage and making lots of models

In my research there was one chance example of the actual moment of a child's discovery of the joy of painting. He was captured on the radio microphone. It all happened on one of those dreaded days in settings for young children, when the rain pours down and the children stay inside for 'wet play'. This child chose to set up an easel to paint. I watched him meticulously prepare all his own materials. By four and a half he had become very independent and confident. This was his first day at 'Big School' and he talked non-stop to his long-suffering teacher as he painted. 'This is my favourite thing! This is my very favourite thing!' Suddenly he stopped. He had noticed that when the paint dribbles ran into each other, the colour changed. He sang as he experimented further:

All of my work. I got orange. Yellow dripping down again ... but red now ... orange ... ORANGE ... Oh, it's dripping on my red now, it's all gone yucky ... All yellow, all yellow now ... yellow more yellow ... some yellow on the red ... ORANGE some more ... some more yellow on some blue ... green ... GREEN. Look teacher, look what I done there! Teacher, I've done another one down there.

Choosing art materials

Unlike that child mixing his paint, only at very few settings did the children mix their own paints or make their own choice of brush sizes. Many children also said they did not like the way the paint dribbled down the upright easel and commented 'it dribbles all over and makes it all messy ... yuk!' They did not like anything messy and said: 'We'll get in trouble if we get paint on our clothes.' Some commented that they 'like drawing and felt-tips the best', but they too were worried about it 'staining my fingers ... it won't even come off'. All the settings had overalls and old shirts for the children to wear, but many of them could not be persuaded to paint regularly. That was quite different from young children in the more creatively orientated 'family arts workshops' in which I am actively involved.

Apart from a few isolated cases, the painting I have observed in a variety of settings was closely linked to a theme or to an event being celebrated, or to adding a contribution to a group mural. Paper was cut to size ready for use and brushes were limited in both size and texture. Sometimes, large and small sponges had been added to the resources but rarely did the children have water and containers to mix their own paints and experiment with them. When they did, the effect on the children was immediate. They were animated and enthusiastic and the quality of the work they produced was outstanding. They told me how much they enjoyed painting. Their spontaneous experimentation with colours was very different from the more stylised and sterile pictures which many settings had on their walls. One sensitive child told me:

I love printing with the sponges because when you lift them up you leave a pattern or a space. I look at the spaces and sometimes they look like white clouds ... and sometimes when it's all different blues and greens it's like under the sea. I would choose printing every day but sometimes we can't have that. We have different things and we choose them instead. I suppose if I asked I could print.

Another similarly sensitive boy had been heard comparing a painting he had seen in a gallery with a Japanese print on a calendar on the wall of his setting. His expression was poetic: 'It was a bit like a painting ... soft and delicate ... feathery like clouds in the sky.' Like the little girl mentioned earlier who had to adjust to two settings (see p. 38), those more creative children who had experience of artistic activities at home seemed initially confused that they were 'not allowed to choose'.

Some of the children were able to express what art meant to them. In their own words, they also explained the importance of being free to choose what to do or what to make. This was confirmed by a girl of almost five:

I really didn't want to make a Mother's Day card with cut-out flowers. All of us had to make a picture like that. I didn't want to and I started to cry, then Miss said I could make a fluffy cat if I wanted ... no, I didn't fancy a cat so I never made a cat neither. I wanted to draw my mum a house. Miss said 'Yes, alright then, but you'll be the only one without pretty flowers.' I drawed a house. It was a really beautiful ... that's my favourite thing drawing houses.

With collage, the opportunity to choose was very rare indeed. That medium was used more to extend awareness of the local environment or to capture features such as stained-glass windows and church architecture. There appeared to be an excessive use of crumpled tissue paper. It was difficult to see how it could represent so many different things. Observation showed it was used for pebbles, walls, flower petals, leaves, butterfly wings and even people. One child muttered to me: 'I *hate* tissue! it's all squishy and gluey ... Ugh! It don't even look like nothing!' That was the problem, it did look and feel like nothing except crumpled-up pieces of tissue. That child had a highly discriminating eye and a strong sense of the aesthetic.

Collage was more popular for some children but it was seldom used individually from the imagination. Frequently an outline had been drawn by the staff and groups of children chose different textured materials from a box or tub and stood there sticking them on. The material was already cut into small pieces ready for use. When these fabrics were used for collage it seemed as though the scientific aspects were more important than their creative use, for example whether those materials were equally 'waterproof' or whether they could be secured with glue.

Even where clay existed it was rarely used. The lack of understanding of its properties and expressive and developmental potential was widespread. When I looked in most clay bins, the clay was rock hard and frequently covered in waste paper. Some of the children talked about having clay in the garden 'sometimes in the summer' and described how they used it 'with lots and lots of water, then we all take off our clothes and teacher sprays us down with the hose … Lovely fun!' Now we were really getting somewhere. Fun with clay, perhaps there is room for some optimism after all. Three-dimensional work generally was neglected.

Junk modelling was in evidence and used mainly by boys. Many of them declared they 'make lots of models'. Most of the girls were singularly uninterested in three-dimensional work with junk. However, some girls did enjoy making sculptural forms with off-cuts of scrap wood and glue. Working with wood in other ways was often considered by the adults to be 'too dangerous with tools; imagine saws and hammers with younger children around'. There were some settings where the potential of 'real tools' and child choice and experimentation were recognised as educationally very valuable. Often, for safety, a mother sat near the tools and helped the children when necessary. In each case those mothers intuitively sensed frustration and knew when to lend a helping hand.

When children were given such rich opportunities to experiment and to take risks as they learned, they talked about it to me in a very excited way. As one said:

Look at our wood. We've got a work bench and proper … look a real hammer … a little saw and nails. You got to put it in a vice … Look! I made a car but I never made wheels … wheels … round wheels are hard! Mum says to cut up a broom handle … she's going to find an old handle to make the wheels.

Whatever happened to playing with paint?

The tradition of adults supporting creative activities appears to have diminished in many early years settings. In the course of this research, many people have told me they are too overloaded with other curriculum demands and excessive paperwork. That tradition of adults working alongside children is still very strong in family and community arts events. Over the years, adults organising other family arts workshops have told me how many of their young participants lacked confidence and said to them: 'I'm bad at art. I can't draw, I can't paint … I'm useless at it.' I have found this being said by children as young as four in many of the settings I visited in the course of my research. This may be a fear transmitted by the adults. So few children chose art activities as their favourite in my research. Their reasons appeared to be associated more with not being allowed to make their own choices or to experiment with various materials and be able to freely express themselves. Some of the adults in their settings complained about having no time for creative art. 'There's no room for it anyway!' was commonly heard.

As I have written earlier, every surface and flat space in the settings was filled. A strong tradition of my early days as a playgroup mum and then as a nursery teacher seemed to have gone. We were always able to leave an empty table in the room for the children to set up their own choice of a creative activity, for self-expression and experimentation. If we did not have a table we spread a large sheet on the floor and they used that. Art has now become an area to set up (or not) by adults for their own convenience. Blame is not attributed to them because most of them were similarly deprived of art in their own education.

The fate of music and dance is even worse. Apart from settings which had retained the fundamental conviction that music and dance are important and had initiated arts events with stimulating and committed groups, there was even less experimental dance and music-making. Is it really possible that the visual and performing arts have been so marginalised? Has the swing back to basics neglected what is so very basic for the healthy development of young children?

Until I visited all those settings and listened to all those children, I had taken it for granted that children of four would still have the opportunity to choose to paint or play with clay, make music, or dance and sing. That is what comes naturally to them; it is what they have always done. In Britain we used to have a tradition where children aged three could choose the texture of their paper. They cut it to size, *their* size, using a creasing technique and the back of a blunt knife. They spent long periods of time in carefully pouring paint into palettes, experimenting with colour mixing and getting water to rinse the brushes they had selected by themselves. I can see them now with their patty tins of paint and small flat sponges used to dab their brushes dry before they busily dipped them into different colours. They often expressed themselves with little blobs and splashes of colour or patches of patterned paint. Sometimes they would paint a recognisable picture of 'my mum' which described all her main features. Later, that would be placed proudly on a kitchen wall.

I know and celebrate the fact that real art still happens in some settings but in my research, two-dimensional and three-dimensional art as a free and creative voice for the children has become rare. Since the late 1970s the educational system has consistently destroyed the arts and, apart from a few voices in the wilderness, society has allowed it to happen.

The reasons are immaterial. I certainly have serious concerns about Ofsted's intentions and whether the arts really are valued as part of lifelong learning. A 'top-down' approach to national curriculum design and implementation has already had a profound effect on the curriculum for children aged four. Unless there is considerable change, this lack of emphasis on artistic and creative involvement will continue to deprive children of emotional well-being. We all have current examples of very young children with very poor self-esteem. It is now known that such deprivation is even more serious in hindering their thinking. Current research has also shown that the age of four (or thereabouts) marks a significant stage in the development of the brain and its link to the emotions.

In my research into the favourite things of those 130 children aged four, opportunities for children to make their own discoveries and express their own feelings have been high on their agenda. Their talking has shown how powerful is the effect of personal choice in encouraging their strongest motivation and their deepest level of thought. Their talking has also revealed some of the secrets of their often troubled lives and provides increasing evidence that so many of our young children are suffering emotionally because of breakdowns in loving and stable relationships between the adults in their lives. Without a sustaining engagement with the arts, how else will they be able to externalise such pain?

3 Observing four year olds

There are many ways of carrying out observations and all of them tell their different stories about the children by focusing on different things in different ways. None of the examples given here should be regarded as prescriptive. They are included to share some of the often simple ways in which staff in a variety of settings manage the crucial art of observation. An increasing number of settings have begun to adopt developmental approaches to observation. They do not attempt to compartmentalise either the children or their learning but emphasise the inter-connectedness of much which they observe. For example, they are more likely to note aspects of the child's mood or include other background information that could be having an effect upon the child.

Other settings have adopted an approach to the observation of natural patterns in the children's play known as 'schemas'. Based on the work of Jean Piaget in the 1960s, the various schemas can be interpreted by informed observers as they watch the children's play. They are then reassured that some seemingly obsessional and repeated patterns in their behaviour (such as wrapping everything up, including the cat) are perfectly normal. They also help the adults to make sure that the children have plenty of suitable materials to develop thoroughly through the various stages which their playing reflects.[24]

Whichever approach to observation is chosen, the specific focus or concerns about the children often determine the amount of detail to be included in any written observations. Not all observations need to be added to the children's records – that would be an arduous and unnecessary burden with large numbers of children. Some observations providing snapshots of a brief moment in the life of the child are enough, while others need longer to go into greater detail and to be repeated over a period of time.

Prolonged observations

The observation of young children is often a team matter, and is one of the reasons many reception teachers in my research gave for not being able to observe. They were often either alone in the class with 30 children or they had an assistant for only part of each day.

---

24 For full details of this fascinating observational approach and the theory behind it see Bruce, T. (1997) *Child care and education*, Hodder and Stoughton.

Why do prolonged observation?

Shedi often shouted at the other children, especially at a cousin who was in another group. Normally Shedi was a very amiable and docile child, so it was puzzling. She was unable to explain what the problem was and her behaviour was distracting others. Her keyworker had observed this behaviour from the start of the day till after the children had become engaged with their first activities, which was over 15 minutes.

By using a prolonged observation technique over three days, the keyworker was able to identify Shedi's specific difficulty. On three occasions she was 'sparked off' by her cousin who, on Day 1 of the observation, took Shedi's favourite doll, on Day 2 stuck her tongue out at Shedi and called her a rude name, and on Day 3 pushed Shedi when she thought nobody was looking.

With the identification of the problem complete, it was soon sorted out. Young children often have a very strong sense of justice and once Shedi knew that her keyworker had found out what the problem was she was able to ignore the taunts of her cousin – which did not cease completely, but gradually faded.

Observation takes time and preparation and it also takes concentration, especially when listening to what the child is saying.

When working a keyworker system, staff frequently took responsibility for the incidental and spontaneous observations of their children and also observed all their children systematically in a variety of contexts.

Spontaneous observations

In most settings, these were written in note form in a small observation notebook kept in the pocket of each member of staff. Each entry tracked individual children or group interactions and followed this format:
- date;
- code or initials instead of names (where appropriate, to maintain the confidentiality of the children);
- context in which the observation took place, for example 'playing outside';
- dialogue, if it added to the observation or illustrated a point;
- comments about the child's/children's involvement and interest level;
- any particular surprises, for example use of language or mathematical concepts;

- a section entitled 'I need to', where key parts of the observation would be identified for transfer to children's records or to note information for future planning; and
- a final section entitled 'Must help with', to make note of more urgent help needed by any particular child.

Example taken from an observation notebook

Date 2 February

Context JF playing with small group outside with wheeled toys

Observation Noticed how happy JF has been to play with PL. They seem to have reached an understanding about taking turns with the tractor. Very imaginative substitution of the construction kit to become spanners to tighten the wheels. Sustained conversations throughout, eg JF suggested 'going for a mechanic now' and was happy to have PU join in as one of the new mechanics. PL explained that the tyre kept going flat but the wheel seemed loose. Good vocabulary.

I need to update PL's language record and add some of their new words to their 'garage chart', eg spanners, nuts and bolts.

Must help with PU needs to play more with the construction set; hard for him to hold small bolts.

Systematic observations

Most settings had developed (or were in the process of developing) their own schedules of observation. Some of these used Ofsted's framework of the six curriculum areas and broke those down into developmental steps or stages which they thought were appropriate. The following framework was developed by ten reception teachers and myself as a result of some action research carried during 1986. I later adapted it again for all curriculum areas and varied the lengths of observations.

In our schedules we often changed places as observer and teacher. Families joined in the various observations and it was interesting to compare how the children's talk varied with different people. It was also enlightening to record how many interruptions the children and staff endured in the course of a day and how many pointless questions we all asked. In recent years many of the items on that schedule have been greatly simplified as part of the development of my professional practice and thinking. As natural constructivists, we in the early years sector can learn for ever.

Oral language observation schedule

Date 3 April

Time 9.30 (after settling in large group) until 9.55

Name of child Peter

Reason child has been chosen for observation Very shy and not talking in the large group; Chris concerned because he doesn't seem to talk anywhere in school. Observed by Jacqui as early years support teacher and research facilitator.

Context of observation Moving into a smaller group with Alice (classroom assistant) to choose an activity.

Context set up by Peter.

What is the child doing? 9.30 Looking carefully through all the boxes. Seems to know what he wants to play with.

Engaged in the activity or not? To what extent? Peter has found the smaller lego with the longer boards and started to build a garage with a sloping roof. He is very interested and engaged in the activity.

What part is the child playing with other children? eg passive onlooker, listening, energetic participant, leader Peter asked Dave and Lynne to help him find the roof parts. He explained that he is building a garage and is acting as a leader, checking that the parts are securely fitted together.

Evidence of child's attitudes, eg curious, engaged or very involved, concentrating, trying or persevering, bored At the end of ten minutes, Peter is still very engaged and enthusiastic about this activity.

Comments on child's behaviour or mood Shy with Alice and did not refer to her, but happy and enthusiastic throughout the activity.

What role is the adult playing? eg managerial, interrupting or being interrupted, listening, or alongside Supportive, watchful, helping child choose a book, letting Peter play without interruption.

Child talking in this context? Yes, to his friends. Giving them instructions clearly, using his imagination and making up a story about a car going for its MOT.

Is talk relevant in this context? Yes, because he has drawn others into the game.

Any noticeable features of child's language? Very clear and mature.

Any other thoughts for ways forward for this child or adults? Peter talks well. Suggest continue in the same way by allowing plenty of free choice. Compared with observation in larger group, he looked much happier and relaxed. Only a matter of time before he is drawn in to contribute, he was so involved and excited and showed Alice the model they made. Alice WONDERFUL! Put it on 'interest table' immediately: perhaps he'll share it later?

4 Giving four year olds a chance

Let them develop at their own pace

Many of us in early years care and education have worked for more than 25 years in collaborative partnerships within various networks of people from all agencies and in various areas of early childhood study. Such networks of knowledge provide many forums for the kind of discussion that is beginning to break down some of the traditional barriers between different professionals, whether in the statutory or non-statutory sectors. In our learning process, we acknowledge the crucial importance of listening to the children themselves and to their families. It is only they who can voice how they really feel. That voice may be expressed through language, but with young children it has been seen through the Reggio Emilia experience how their voices might be better expressed through the arts.[25]

A more rounded picture of young children's whole and healthy development is now being gained which is helping us to keep a watchful and informed eye on them. It is through such discussion with colleagues that we now know more about the critical phases of maturation and development which the brain passes through. It is that growing body of research which most powerfully points to the futility of trying to hurry up the development of our young children.

Negative attitudes about young children seem to have become firmly embedded in our national psyche. Unlike Sonnyboy, we seem to have forgotten how young four really is. Pressure must be taken off and much more support and study given to educators so that they can allow their children and themselves time 'to be'. They will then be able to better organise their play and creative activities so that the 'WOW!' of being four is restored. Deep questioning and high-quality learning will occur as part of that process.

Making a future for our children

Listening to the wisdom of our children of 'only four' has given me very great optimism. At arts workshops that I help to run in Devon, the children express themselves with many voices and have wonderful

---

25 Reggio Emilia (1996) *The hundred languages of children*, book accompanying Reggio Emilia exhibition.

visions for the future. They feel strongly about 'being with friends and loving them' and 'thinking about all the hungry people'. More than that, they know about 'imagining and having parties and bringing all the hungry kids and, well, doing something about it!' Isn't that the key to being visionary? The imagination of our young children is still there despite the 'delerious somefins'. We adults need to release them to let their vision fly; the millennium is their future.

If our young children of four are going to realise their vision for a fairer future then we too need to take action and design an agenda for a visionary new millennium, that:

■ values childhood in its own right and not as a preparation for adulthood;

■ acknowledges the value of all families as the prime educators of their children; and

■ reinforces the need to regard everybody who cares for and educates young children (including all their families) as specialists of equal worth, with many minds but one voice speaking to policymakers on behalf of young children.

To do this, we will need to:

■ draw on the diversity of early years families, carers and educators rather than wasting time and energy on 'territorial' issues and reduction of that diversity;

■ support high-quality early years inter-agency partnerships that have already been initiated nationally and put into practice imaginatively and successfully;

■ support existing and effective befriending or parenting projects within communities, and initiate more projects where none exist;

■ encourage everyone who works with young children to gain access to recognised qualifications and lifelong in-service training, which includes examination of their own practice and the study of early child development, including the observation of young children in their own settings;

■ challenge political and bureaucratic divisiveness, and share funding more equally;

■ challenge those who seek to 'marginalise by ridicule' the rigorous research of those whose specialism is of children in their early years; and

■ raise the status of early years practitioners by paying them adequately and enabling more of them to take part in specialist courses and action research projects as part of broader early years 'networks of knowledge'.

It is essential that we do this and that we take control of our own agenda for the development and learning of young children. For their sake, we must be released from the constraints of the current educational system in order to put into practice our firmly held beliefs about young children's education for their 'being' as well as for their 'doing'. Only by focusing more on the children and the holistic and inter-related ways in which they develop, and by withdrawing from superficial outcomes, can we help them become true lifelong learners.